SAY WHAT?

The Origins of Everyday Idioms and Phrases
Explore the Fascinating Histories and Fun Facts Behind the Words We Use

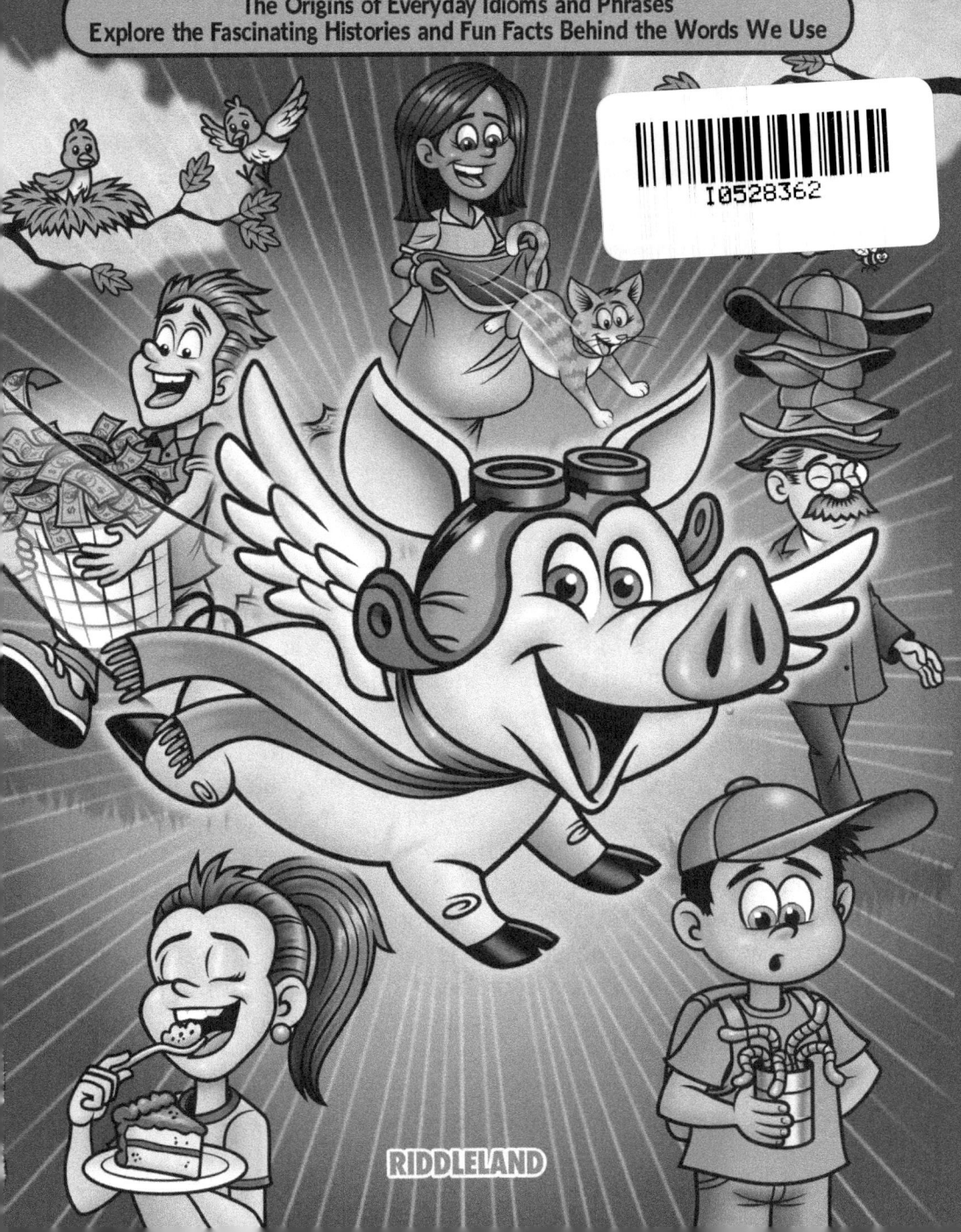

I0528362

RIDDLELAND

INTRODUCTION

What is an Idiom?

Can you make sense of this sentence: My coworkers are dirty rats who stabbed me in the back and threw me under the bus because I chickened out and fell off the wagon?

If you are a native speaker of English above the age of 12, the sentence probably makes perfect sense. If you are a literalist, which most people are until around the age of 12, or if English is a second language, you are probably wondering why the speaker works with rats, how the rats were able to pick up a knife, how they lifted the speaker to the bus stop, and what is so bad about falling from a wagon.

The meaning expressed in this sentence has nothing to do with rats, chickens, knives, buses, or wagons. Instead, it is a way of expressing that one was betrayed by one's friends because one lost one's confidence and returned to one's former habits.

Phrases like "dirty rats", "stabbed in the back," "thrown under the bus," "chickened out", and "fell off the wagon" are idioms. An idiom is a group of words that have a specific meaning when they are used together, and what the idiom means may be very different from what any of the words mean separately.

Idioms are expressions passed from generation to generation and often mean something very different than their literal meaning. Idioms are used to set a mood and often mean something that no English word can convey. Natural speakers of English tend to recognize these phrases and know what they mean; non-native speakers and children often struggle with idioms, which make no sense if taken literally. Also, you have to pity the non-native speaker, for these idioms are culture-specific in most cases, so if you ever translate an English work into Spanish, German, Japanese, Russian, or whatever language you prefer, you cannot quote the idiom word for word or it will make absolutely no sense.

Although most native speakers of English use idioms properly, few can tell you how most idioms originated. For instance, most English speakers know that "I'm joshing you" means that I am not telling you the full truth; however, very few people could identify the Josh who inspired the phrase or explain why the "J" in josh is not capitalized. This book answers those questions - who was Josh and why "joshing" is written with lowercase "J" - and elaborates upon the background of 49 other idioms that are very popular in today's culture.

This book is designed to be a fun read; whether you are a fan of history, grammar, pop culture, or trivia, you are likely to enjoy this book. Each chapter is based on an idiom, providing its meaning, history, and fun facts about its topics. Most chapters begin with an engaging question that will inspire you to think critically, laying the foundation for you to research idioms not included in this book. Not only will your vocabulary grow, but so will your understanding of how we got this crazy, sometimes nonsense-sounding language of English. The idioms are listed in alphabetical order, and at the back, an index is provided that lists all idioms explained in the book, even if the idiom does not have its own chapter. You can read the book cover to cover, enjoying all fifty stories; you can also use it as a reference guide to find the meaning of an idiom you hear but don't recognize. This is one book you are likely to return to again and again.

Although it is rare, idioms can be both figurative and literal. Don't you believe me? I am about to use an idiom that means "to move on," yet, in this case, it is to be taken literally – let's turn the page.

TABLE OF CONTENTS

CHAPTER 1

AGE BEFORE BEAUTY

MEANING
The older person should go first.

HOW IT CAME TO BE

What happens when two objects want to occupy the same space simultaneously? It is a physical impossibility, and the two objects slam into each other, damaging one another and causing debris to fly.

Fortunately, our governments have given some thought to the fact that two objects will likely want the same spot at the same time. For instance, in the United States, if two cars arrive at a four-way intersection simultaneously, the car on the right gets to gofirst. Without these rules, the drivers would have to negotiate their own arrangements, or chaos would result.

Just like two drivers may want to occupy the same space, so might two people. For instance, the typical household doorway is big enough for one person to walk through at a time, but when my mom calls for supper, we all want to walk through it simultaneously. The government has not legislated laws to govern social interactions. Although I might get fussed at, told I was rude, and cautioned that I needed to be polite, I am not going to get fined or go to jail because I try to race ahead of someone to get out of a room.

Household doorways are made to fit one person at a time, so what happens when two people want to pass through the narrow entrance simultaneously? There may not have been a law passed by Congress or decree made by the King of England, but the common wisdom passed from generation to generation is "age before beauty". That is, the older of the two should go through the entryway first.

The meaning, though, can change slightly depending on who is saying the idiom. When "age before beauty" is said by an older person to a younger person, the remark reminds the young to bestow honor and privilege upon the elder. Although the elder compliments the younger person's good looks, the elder insists on going first and reprimanding the latter for his lack of manners.

The idiom can be used as a very catty remark. Many women do not want to be known as old, nor do they want to be perceived as ugly. Therefore, if a young woman says "age before beauty" to an older woman, she is, in essence, calling her rival old and ugly while giving the elder woman the right to go through the passageway first. "Old" and "ugly" are not exactly compliments.

"Age before beauty" has never appeared in a book of manners. Books outlining proper social etiquette appeared around 1200 in various European cultures. With the rise of nations, kings had their courts of queens, dukes, and other gentry class members. It was important for each person in court to know how to behave to avoid offending anyone else. The idiom "age before beauty" first appeared in print around 1850.

Although it is said light-heartedly and jokingly, it is sometimes spoken begrudgingly after letting an older person go first. Usually, though, the phrase is generally said in a joking way. For instance, a teen girl might call, "Grandma, hurry up, and you can get in front of me. Age before beauty."

FUN FACTS

Old age and wisdom are said to go together like youth and beauty. Although "age before beauty" questions if wisdom should trump youth, other sayings, such as "Respect your elders," leave no doubt.

A retort to "age before beauty" attributed to both Dorothy Parker and Winston Churchill is "pearls before swine", implying that they will accept the invitation to go first because they are the more important person.

Although originally written for aristocrats, courtesy books on manners found a secondary audience - middle-class citizens who aspired to become aristocrats.

CHAPTER 2

ALL WENT SOUTH

MEANING
It did not go well.

HOW IT CAME TO BE

Have you ever flipped a two-way light switch, turning it up-down, up-down, and up-down? When the switch is in the on position, it is up; when it is in the off position, it is down.

Have you ever read a map legend? If you have, then you know that the north is up, and the south is down. To say that the light switch went south would mean that the light would not turn on.

The concept of "south" being bad can also be found in the "thumbs up/thumbs down" gesture used in society. If I like something, I give it a "thumbs up". If I do not like it, I give it a "thumbs down".

The "thumbs up/thumbs down" gesture originated in the Roman amphitheater. At the end of the battle, the winning fighter would turn to the master of ceremonies and ask if he should kill the loser. (They literally fought to the death in those days.) The crowd would give their input with a thumbs-up or down sign. A thumbs down meant death – crush him like a bug; a thumbs up meant to spare the loser.

The loser got a thumbs up if he had done a good job. Around 1600, the gesture surfaced in everyday European life. Whereas some gestures are innate – for instance, everyone smiles when they are happy; that is a natural human gesture – other gestures are learned. The thumbs up/thumbs down gesture is learned. Because it is a learned gesture, though, where one culture might use a "thumbs up" for good, another culture might use a "thumbs down" for good. Around 1900 in the United States, the meaning that we have today – a thumb pointing up/northward is a sign of contentment, and a thumb pointing down/southward is a sign of disapproval – became set.

FUN FACTS

On compasses, the north is always up.

If you were to drop an item, it would go south, down toward the earth's surface. An item "going south" is on the verge of "hitting rock bottom;" rock bottom is where things cannot get any worse.

Although "going south" is a recognized idiom, "going north" is not.

CHAPTER 3

BACK TO THE DRAWING BOARD

MEANING
Something went wrong with our plan, and we have to fix it.

HOW IT CAME TO BE

Pause for a moment and think about the rooms in your house. How did you choose their name and function? Our home has a "game room" where we play games. My grandma has a "sewing room" where she sews and stores all her sewing equipment. My dad enjoys electric trains, so we have a "train room" where he tinkers.

For about 400 years, upper-class homes often contained a "drawing room." As the name suggests, drawings were made in that room. The drawings might be a diagram of how something would go together or a house blueprint. Before computers and the invention of computer-drafting-and-design software programs, blueprint drawings were made by hand on a drawing board.

The drawing board was first constructed around 1600. It was made from wood and brass and therefore was out of most people's price range; this piece of furniture belonged in the homes of the wealthy. A drawing table was a sign of status; to show off that status, the entire room was often named in its honor – the drawing room. Those lower-upper middle class who could still afford a drawing board but did not have a room to devote to it would place the drawing table in a study or a library.

Drawing boards are different from ordinary tables in two ways. One, the top tilts so that it can be at any angle. Two, the bottom of the table has a small ledge that maintains the paper and holds pencils.

Although the drawing board was invented around 1600, the slogan "back to the drawing board" did not originate until the early 1940s. With the outbreak of World War II, both sides were looking for the next generation of weapons so they could have an edge. Artists would do their best drawing and then give the drawing to the contractor, who would attempt to build the project. Sometimes what worked on paper did not work in reality, so the architect would have to go back to the drawing board to make corrections and new plans. Having to make new plans and "go back to the drawing board" became synonyms.

FUN FACTS

A New Yorker cartoon may have inspired this phrase. In 1941, Peter Arno drew a picture of a man looking at plane wreckage, saying, "Well, back to the drawing board."

Drawing on a flat table means that the angle one is drawing from differs from the angle that one has seen one's subject matter; that's why drawing tables and easels hold the paper at an angle instead of sitting flat.

CHAPTER 4

THE BALL IS IN YOUR COURT

MEANING
You have got to act now that somebody else has taken action.

HOW IT CAME TO BE

This idiom's success is due to television!

Although the idiom "the ball is in your court" has nothing to do with television - it has to do with tennis; if it weren't for the invention of the television, the idiom would likely not have caught on in popular culture to the degree it has.

Have you ever seen a tennis court and witnessed games of tennis? If you have, you know that the game consists of either one-versus-one or two-versus-two. A net separates the sides; it is three feet tall at its lowest point and 3 ½ feet tall at its highest point. The game's objective is to hit the ball on your side of the net so that it goes inbounds onto your opponent's side but so that your opponent cannot hit it back to you.

Once the ball has crossed the net, the player on the other side of the court must act; the ball is in that person's court. Until that moment, that person didn't have to do anything. When the ball is present in one's area – the area is referred to as a court, one must spring into action.

In life, we often delegate a task to someone else. Once we delegate it, we are done with it. (A good supervisor, though, will follow up on delegated tasks to make sure they are getting done.) A delegated task is someone else's responsibility. Woe to us, though, if it gets delegated back to us. The other person may claim they don't have the skills or the time to do it; now we have responsibility for the task; the ball is in our court.

Tennis has traditionally been a game of the upper class; the lower class had to farm the land and work the factories. Since it was a game of the upper class, the lower and middle classes had no interest in it. With the rise of television, though, that changed. Tennis became a game that all classes could enjoy watching. The lower and middle classes, who have traditionally not had enough property to set aside for the luxury of playing a game, also found themselves with places to play the game; thanks to the "green space" and "parks and recreation movements," public tennis courts became available for the poor and middle-class. Although the idiom "the ball is in your court" was around in the 1800s, it was seldom heard outside high society. However, with the spread of tennis on television came the spread of the idiom, and by 1970, the phrase was one of the most popular idioms in culture and has remained so to this day.

FUN FACTS

Tennis began around 1100 in France; it wasn't until around 1500 that people used rackets; for over 400 years, people just used their hands to smack the ball.

Early tennis balls in France contained wool inside them; in England, they contained human hair.

Television influenced modern tennis in many ways; for instance, the traditional white tennis ball was replaced with fluorescent yellow balls because the television audience could follow the fluorescent yellow balls easier – which meant they were more inclined to watch the game.

CHAPTER 5

BANG YOUR HEAD AGAINST A WALL

MEANING
To engage passionately in a seemingly lost cause.

HOW IT CAME TO BE

Although there are exceptions in some cultures, most humans are free to marry whomever they want. Certain rituals have been established so couples can see if they mesh well enough for marriage. If two people believe they have mutual appeal, they will go on a few dates. The first date generally involves finding out about the other person, and future dates allow the couple to address specifics, such as child-rearing philosophy. If that mutual appeal is confirmed after a series of dates, they will likely settle down. It's not always the strongest, the wittiest, or the richest who gets selected; it is the one with the most appeal who also finds them appealing.

Whereas we humans go on dates, the animal kingdom also has its rituals for mate selection. In the case of cattle and Rocky Mountain goats, the males interested in the women have a contest to see who has greater endurance. They will literally charge at each other with their heads down, attempting to send the other flying. When we "bang heads" with somebody at a business meeting, we remind others how those two creatures charge at one another.

Banging one's head into a wall is similar in meaning. However, instead of charging at a second person, one simply puts one's head down and runs full force toward a wall. A brick wall is solid, and no matter how often one headbutts it, the wall is not likely to fall. Therefore, banging your head against a wall is perceived as a futile use of time. The headbanger will likely end up with a headache and maybe a concussion, a reputation for being stubborn and foolish simultaneously, and have accomplished nothing worthwhile. Since the 1880s, the brick wall has symbolized something impassable or immovable. People were said to "hit a brick wall" when they encountered a major problem, such as obtaining financing for a project.

Notice the words "not likely to fall" and "perceived as a futile use of time". Banging one's head against the wall may be something that other people expect to fail, which they consider a waste of time, but to the person doing the banging, it may be worthwhile. I have seen brick walls that have fallen; brick walls do come down. Although "banging your head against the wall" shows futility, if you want to "be the change," you must butt some walls. Whereas in the 1880s, brick walls were symbols of immovable things, in our more optimistic society, brick walls have become symbolic of things that are frustrating, annoying, and exasperating but, with due diligence, might be overcome.

FUN FACTS

The oldest brick was made about 9500 years ago in Mesopotamia along the Tigris River, made from straw and mud.

Over 3.8 billion bricks comprise The Great Wall of China.

Red bricks get their coloring from the iron they contain.

CHAPTER 6

BARKING UP THE WRONG TREE

MEANING
Getting the wrong idea or reaching the wrong conclusion.

HOW IT CAME TO BE

Have you ever played Hide and Seek? In the version of Hide and Seek that my friends and I usually played, one person closed their eyes and counted to 100 while the rest hid. Once at 100, the counter would try to find where everyone had scattered. When the counter found one, that person, too, became a seeker. The last person to be found became the new counter.

In our version, the hiding person did not have to stay in one hiding place. That person could move around and could even hide in a spot where the seeker had looked previously. It was a goodstrategy, but it was not original. In the wild, prey sometimes does this when a predator intensely hunts it.

For instance, if the beagle Bubba sees a raccoon going through the trashcan in his owner's backyard, Bubba will chase it. As the beagle approaches, the raccoon will scamper to safety, usually jumping onto a tree and climbing up it. Bubba, of course, can't climb, so he will stay at the bottom of the tree barking until his owner comes over to see what the noise is about. Bubba will proudly look up into the tree, expecting to see the raccoon cowering there.

However, a clever raccoon will not be in that tree when Bubba and his owner look up. Although Bubba will have eliminated the option to climb down the tree trunk, the clever raccoon will have snuck out of the tree by jumping unseen limb-to-limb into another tree. Thus, Bubba is barking up the wrong tree.

Like Bubba, people sometimes try to point out answers to others. These know-it-all people may be adamant in what they are saying, just like Bubba barking at the base of a tree, and just like Bubba, they can be wrong. Since the 1830s, when people have adamantly pointed to the wrong answer, they are said to be barking up the wrong tree.

FUN FACTS

Raccoons are not just rural animals. Because trashcans and dumpsters provide a ready food supply, many raccoons favor urban life. Toronto, Canada, has one of the largest urban raccoon populations.

A human nose has approximately five million scent receptors; a bloodhound's nose has 300 million scent receptors.

To crawl down from a tree head-first, a raccoon will turn its back feet 180 degrees.

CHAPTER 7

BE A FLY ON THE WALL

MEANING
To hear but not be observed.

HOW IT CAME TO BE

Do you get nervous when your boss is watching you? Do you behave differently when your parents are watching you than when your friends are watching you? Most of us do. Many people get pretty rowdy on Saturday night with their friends, but they appear as little angels when they are with their family on Sunday morning. People behave differently when they know they are being watched.

Before I go further, I want you to answer this question: Have you been annoyed by a fly today? If it is midsummer, the chances are that you have. Flies tend to like to eat the same foods we like to eat – as well as rotten fruit, manure, and a lot of things that we don't like to eat, and so they buzz around us trying to get to our food. (Most of us do not willingly share with the flies.) Not only do we have the food they want, but in the case of female horseflies, we are the food; these giant flies need horse and human blood for extra nutrients to assist with egg laying.

For every fly that harasses us, there is probably another fly quietly biding its time on the wall. Because this fly is quiet, no one pays it any attention. Those who see it assume it is a speck of dust and then ignore it. This fly can hear and see everything, but it is so inconspicuous that no one pays it any attention.

To "be a fly on the wall" means to be in a room with someone so that you can hear and see the action but not be noticed by the participants. Since the participants do not know they are being watched, they will behave "naturally". The idiom "be a fly on the wall" first appeared in print in 1921 in an Oakland, California, newspaper. It has remained a popular part of culture

FUN FACTS

Flies carry almost two million types of bacteria.

Flies do not have teeth. The acid from the vomit breaks down the food and allows the fly to suck up the food as a liquid.

Flies really do vomit on your food if they land on it.

CHAPTER 8

BEAT AROUND THE BUSH

MEANING
To speak in a round-about, indirect way rather than to bluntly come out and say something.

HOW IT CAME TO BE

Have you ever gone hiking to try to get a glimpse of quail?

Quail are chubby birds, and they are found on every continent except Antarctica. If you have never seen one and live near farmland, it is likely because they are so good at hiding. If you want to find one, you need to flush it out. You need to beat around the bush, literally.

Why not hit the bush directly with a stick to flush it out? One, the bush may have a nest of bees inside it, and they won't behappy with your disturbing them. Two, if you were to hit the bush, you might hurt the quail. Instead of directly hitting the bush, it is wise to beat around it.

Beating around the bush is also a life-saving technique. For instance, if you knew that a wild boar was in a bush, you would want to beat around it to flush it out and get it to move off your property. Directly going into the bush where you suspected the wild boar was resting would be foolish, for it would attack you with its razor-sharp tusks.

Many times in life, an indirect approach is a good approach. For instance, if you just saw a dog chew up your sister's homework assignment, you might not want to tell her that bluntly. Instead, you might gradually lead into it, asking, "You love the family dog, don't you?" Likewise, if you broke a window when playing baseball, you might be hesitant to tell your dad what you had done, but, knowing that you shouldn't keep it hidden, you would approach the subject indirectly. Whenever we avoid tough conversations, we are beating around the bush.

However, being around the bush in everyday conversation is not always a good thing. Sometimes the other person will not pick up our hints or recognize the clues we have dropped. Sometimes we procrastinate when we beat around the bush, putting off the tough conversation when we need to have it and get it over with simply. I know that we didn't beat around the bush when discussing "beat around the bush."

FUN FACTS

Bushes are often planted close together to form a natural fence; this row of bushes is called a hedgerow.

Some gardens, called shrubberies, consist of just bushes.

Some bushes change colors with the seasons; others are green year-round.

Quails may be plump and not fly far at any one time, but when they do fly, they fly fast, often reaching twelve miles per hour.

CHAPTER 9

BLOCKBUSTER

MEANING
Something extravagant and hugely successful.

HOW IT CAME TO BE

Are the streets in your town named logically? In my hometown, we had a Main Street, which was literally the main street. Other streets were named after famous people, such as "Grant" Street for Ulysses Grant and "Washington" Street for George Washington; some were named for their current residents, such as "Dustin's Circle; for noted scenery that the street passed, such as "Oak Street"; or for the shape of the street, such as "Circle Drive".

Many towns have a much more logical approach to naming streets. For instance, in Washington, D.C., and many other towns, there is a First Street, Second Street, Third Street, and so forth as one works one's way from left to right. I like the design of Washington, D.C., streets because the cross streets are named with letters, such as "A", "B", "C", and so forth. Therefore, if I need to get to the corner of Fifth and E and I am on Third and D, I know I need to go two blocks over and one block up. In my hometown, there is no logic for getting from Washington to Circle Drive.

Many urban planners use grids with streets running parallel and perpendicular to each other every 400 to 600 feet long. These squares are true "blocks". Other towns, though, are built piecemeal, one piece at a time, and they have rivers and other natural markings, so their "blocks" are not literal blocks but are still islands amid an ocean of asphalt.

When the term "blockbuster" was first used, these were the kinds of blocks that were getting busted. World War II was raging in 1945, and planes on both sides dropped bombs on the other side's towns. A successful bomb with the strength to bring down a city block was called a "blockbuster" by the press. "Blockbuster bombs" were literal block busters. "Blockbuster" came to mean something that was both extravagant and very successful.

After World War II, the term found its way into civilian life, and anything, particularly books, and movies, that were successful were called "blockbusters." The 1975 movie Jaws is considered the first modern blockbuster because it raked in record profits, and people stood in lines for blocks to get into the theater to see it. With the idiom "blockbuster" now beginning to refer to great movies, in 1985, a nationwide chain of video rentals named itself Blockbuster Video. People have associated films with blockbusters ever since. Who knows, maybe this book will become a blockbuster!

FUN FACTS

At its peak in 1994, Blockbuster Video had 9,094 stores; today, one franchise store is all that is left.

The "blockbuster bomb" was also known as "the cookie" by the British Royal Air Force.

Blockbuster bombs dropped in World War II by the British Royal Air Force did not always explode; as recently as 2018, one was discovered in Paderborn, Germany.

CHAPTER 10

BREAK THE ICE

MEANING

To become acquainted and make one feel welcome and relaxed in a group setting.

HOW IT CAME TO BE

Have you ever gone to a rock concert?

If you have, you know that a secondary group usually performs before the main group performs. =The purpose of this secondary group is to get the audience warmed up, that is, in the mood for the main group. =This secondary group performing on stage before the main group is one example of "ice-breaking" in modern society.

Another example of modern "ice-breaking" is when a group of strangers gathers for a meeting. The leader will often arrange for a game or a time of refreshments so people can mingle and get to know one another. People feel awkward and uncomfortable around strangers, so "icebreakers" are used to make people feel welcome. This uncomfortableness creates an icy feeling; the icebreaker is designed to remove this bad vibe and to whet one's appetite for what is coming.

The terms "icebreaker" and "break the ice" originated in the 1500s when small boats would break the ice for bigger boats. Once the small boats had cut through the ice and moved the busted chunks aside, big boats could proceed through the frozen wasteland. Today, a small act or game helps break the figurative ice for the main act. The icebreaker is not the reason people come together, but it plays an important role in ensuring the main act accomplishes its goals.

It's not just rock groups and professional speakers who break the figurative ice; so can you. Rather than just walking up to a prospective customer and saying, "Do you want to buy my company's product?" Or, approaching a romantic interest you have only admired from afar and saying, "Do you want to get married?" you will likely want to break the ice with a simple question – if you look back, you'll see that I did that with this article – a joke or a story to get their interest. Icebreakers put people at ease and make them more receptive to the following main message.

FUN FACTS

In addition to breaking the ice, icebreakers and tugboats can also push or pull stalled boats, be used to help put out fires on bigger boats, and guide boats into the harbor.

The thickness of river ice varies greatly, even in the same river. The ice may be an inch thick in one spot and two feet thick a few feet later (this is why you should never walk on an icy patch of water, because you can't tell the thickness of it and could fall through!)

If you have ever seen a hot knife cut through butter, you have seen how easily especially designed ice-breaking ships can cut through Arctic ice.

CHAPTER 11

BUTTER ME UP

MEANING

To flatter or to be overly nice for selfish reasons, to give false praise, or to do something to win favor.

HOW IT CAME TO BE

Do you believe in a higher being?

In our scientific age, we sometimes forget that almost all primitive societies believed in beings higher than themselves; beings that controlled the weather could decide wars and perform other god-like functions. Some societies were monotheistic, believing in one God, but most were polytheistic, believing in many gods.

To have good crops, to win wars, and to have many children meant appeasing the god in charge of that particular aspect of one's life. Every god, it seemed, had a preferred way of being worshiped. Some wanted grain offerings; some wanted meat offerings. People gave their very best.

In the case of Vishnu, a Hindu god, it was yellow food. This god craved yellow food, and butter was the cream of the crop (no pun intended). People would bring their butter to Vishnu. The butter was a form of flattery, a manipulation to get what they wanted from him.

Today, people still use flattery to get what they want. The hearer often enjoys the praise so much that she does not realize she is being manipulated. Just as people trying to please a god believe that doing deeds will get the god's favor and cause the god to grant the request that follows the flattery, people try to manipulate other humans with the same technique – "Mom, I did the dishes without being asked; can I go to Gena's house now?" Other times, the flattery is through words of praise – "You are so buff. I love your muscles. Do you think you could help me carry groceries up the stairs?"

FUN FACTS

The first butter was from sheep and goats; cows were not yet domesticated.

Cows are the primary source of butter today. Other animals that give butter are sheep, goats, and yaks.

Butter was not popular with ancient Greeks and Romans; it was considered the food of barbarians.

Norsemen loved butter so much that tubs of butter were placed in their graves so they could take it to the afterlife.

CHAPTER 12

CAUGHT RED HANDED

MEANING
Caught in the act of committing a crime or caught with enough evidence to remove any doubt that one committed the crime.

HOW IT CAME TO BE

Do you remember your mom telling you to wash your hands before dinner when you came inside from playing in dust and dirt? My mom always told us to. She would often inspect to make sure that we had done it too. he would ask us to hold out our hands, and then she would inspect them for dirt. She would even look under our fingernails for signs of our adventures that we had failed to wash off.

My mom was a lot like the police of Scotland in the 1500s. When the Scottish police thought that someone had committed a crime, they would ask to see the suspect's hands. Today we have fingerprint technology and microscopes that can inspect one's hands more thoroughly than they could, but they could – and did - check the hand for traces of the crime.

One of the biggest crimes in the 1500s was chicken stealing. A person would go to a farmer's house and steal livestock to eat. In many cases, the animal would be butchered on the spot. Such butchering, of course, got bloodstains on the hands of the criminal. Therefore, if the police saw the tell-tale sign of blood, the suspect was said to have been caught red-handed. The term originally applied to taking a life, whether of a person or an animal. Today, though, it can be used for any act in which one is caught with evidence, not necessarily blood, that makes a solid case.

Although being caught with blood on one's hands became grounds for prosecution in the 1500s, the idiom "caught red-handed" did not appear until the 1820s. In 1819, the Scottish author Sir Walter Scott used the phrase "taken red-handed" in his classic book Ivanhoe, and the phrase soon became "caught red-handed" in popular culture.

FUN FACTS

Other idioms also mention the color red, but it does not refer to blood or taking lives. For instance:

In "paint the town red," "red" refers to the color of fire, implying destruction. Many times, rowdies who came to town lit bonfires that burned out of control; the bonfires created a reddish glow.

In "red letter day," "red" refers to red text, implying importance. Even today, many calendars have holidays marked in red.

In "to see red," "red" refers to a matador's red cape, implying anger. In reality, bulls are colorblind and are upset by the motion of the moving cape, but the audience easily sees the red, and most of the audience forgets the bull is colorblind.

The hand has around 29 bones; some people have more bones than others.

The reddish color of blood comes mostly from the iron in the hemoglobin.

CHAPTER 13

CHICKEN OUT

MEANING
To be a coward at the last minute.

HOW IT CAME TO BE

How superstitious are you? Do you drop pennies into a well or fountain, make a wish, and sincerely expect that wish to come true? Do you refuse to live on the thirteenth floor of a building? If you spill salt, do you throw a pinch over your shoulder so you don't get into an argument? When you pick straws to see who goes first, do you believe that the shortest straw is drawn by fate?

If you answered "yes" to any of these questions, you can relate to ancient warriors who believed the gods talked to them through animals. Some observations of past animal behavior were scientifically accurate – frogs really do croak more before a rainstorm. Therefore, if frogs were louder than usual, people knew rain was coming.

Of course, just because there was a correlation did not mean that the weather caused the animal response; some of the past "success" of the animals' predictions was merely by chance. Until science could prove otherwise, though, people were prone to accept both the accurate and the inaccurate positive results. One of these coincidences was associated with the chicken. If the sacred chicken ate all its corn on the day the attack was to be made, a general felt confident in proceeding. If the chicken did not eat its food on the day of battle, the general believed it was the gods advising he would not be successful on that day, and so, rather than go into battle, the general would "chicken out." Of course, not everybody believed in this superstition. One who did not was General Claudius Pulcher, the Roman general in the First Punic War; he ignored the chicken's message and lost the Battle of Despana decisively.

To "chicken out" would have been a wise choice, but not going into battle was hurtful to his pride. There is a huge difference between bravery and stupidity. "Chickening out" would have been the best option for General Pulcher, and sometimes it is the best option for us. Most people do not rely on literal chickens today, but they have intuition when something is a bad idea.

The phrase "chicken out" may have roots going back centuries, but it didn't become popular in the United States until the 1930s. No one wants to have their pride hurt - and being called a "chicken" is an insult teens hurl at each other all of the time to egg somebody to do something the person is not comfortable doing, but rather than further brinkmanship, sometimes "chickening out" is the best decision one can make. Chickening out may hurt one's pride, but it is the best choice one can make in many cases.

FUN FACTS

Have you heard the phrase "old biddy"?; it's a derogatory way to speak about an older woman. The term "old biddy" also concerns chickens; a biddy is a contrary hen.

"Chickening out" was a popular idiom in European culture in the 1600s; it faded away and made a comeback in the 1930s to the present day.

Chickens have inspired over 36 other current American idioms -including "spring chicken," a way of referring to a youthful person, and "don't count your chickens before they hatch, a way of reminding someone not to be overconfident" – that have nothing to do with maintaining one's pride.

CHAPTER 14

CUT CORNERS

MEANING

Instead of doing a project as the directions require, one finds a different way to get it done, but this cheaper, faster, or easier method results in a lesser quality product.

HOW IT CAME TO BE

Pause for a minute and take a piece of paper. On that paper, put two dots. Now, connect the two points using the shortest route possible. You drew a line, didn't you? That's because the shortest distance between two points is a line.

City planners, it seems, expect people to walk down the sidewalk to the end where it intersects with another sidewalk, but it's human nature to want to take the shortest, most direct route. Therefore, instead of walking around the edges as the city planners envisioned, people will cut corners and take the most direct route there, even if this means jaywalking across a street.

Pedestrians aren't the only ones to cut corners. The idiom "cut corners" arose in the 1800s because horse-and-carriage drivers would have to "round" a corner instead of making a nice square if they were going too fast. In both the case of pedestrians and drivers, literal corners were cut, risking one's safety in the hopes of getting to one's destination sooner.

Many people cut corners because they think they can bypass unnecessary steps. For instance, when I "read" directions on building a new build-it-yourself piece of furniture, I often don't read every detail like the manufacturer intended; I believe I can jump right into building it.

Cutting corners has its benefits. It can often save time and money. Those who successfully cut corners may be hailed as heroes in the workplace. Cutting corners can be good, and some people value the trait.

On the whole, though, cutting corners is frowned upon by society. Ithough the person who successfully cuts corners may be a hero, those who try and fail have to pay a steep price for not following the outlined process. The traditional routine or the directions one is handed have been tested and found to work, and not following the directions is generally considered foolish. Whether it is literally cutting corners on the roads or figuratively cutting corners on a project at work, one may be taking unnecessary risks that will result in losing one's life or career.

FUN FACTS

Researchers have found that people who are self-centered or egotistical are more likely to cut corners than others.

Other idioms associated with driving a vehicle include:
"backseat driver," a person who gives unwanted advice;
"in the driver's seat," a person who is in control of a project;
"driving blind," when you are in charge but don't have enough information to make a good decision; and
"asleep at the wheel," being in charge but not fully aware of what is happening.

"Cutting corners" originally referred to the corners of a road. Other road-inspired idioms include:
"middle of the road," avoiding extremes;
"down the road," into the future;
"straight and narrow road," law-abiding and/or righteous; and
"on the road to _____," in the process of reaching one's goal.

CHAPTER 15

CUT ME SOME SLACK

MEANING
Give me a break.

HOW IT CAME TO BE

Did your mom tell you not to run with scissors?

Mine told me. . . . and told me and told me. She didn't want me to stab myself if I were to fall. She had other rules about scissors too. For instance, she insisted that I don't walk while cutting, that I always store the scissors with the blade down or away from me, and that I keep the blades pointed at the floor when I walked across the room carrying scissors.

I mention scissors because, as a kid, I thought that slack was a kind of material. After all, "slacks" are what we call nice dress pants. (You've likely heard somebody say, "That's a nice pair of slacks you have.") The idiom, though, is not "cut me some slacks;" it is "cut me some slack," and it has nothing to do with material.

The term "slack" came from the world of sailing ships around 1300. It and the term "lax" both come from the English word for "loose." When the wind suddenly shifted, the rope that kept the sails taut would become loose, and it was referred to as "slack." A rope that was "slack" was not tight. For a boat to be untied from the shore, the rope had to be loose enough to undo the knot; therefore, sailors on shore would have been heard saying, "Give me some slack." When you cut somebody slack, you loosen the restraints around them.

"Slack" became an idiom in 1840 but fell out of use. The term resurfaced in the early 1900s in the form of a "slacker," a lazy person, and "slacking off," not carrying one's share. In the 1930s, "Take up the slack" was a part of popular culture; it was a way to motivate slackers. By the late 1960s, the idiom "Take up the slack" had morphed into "Give me some slack" and continued to evolve into today's "Cut me some slack."

FUN FACTS

The idiom, "Give me a break," means the same thing as "Cut me some slack."

If the right blade of a pair of scissors is up when you open it, the scissors are designed for right-handed people.

Since the 1450s, slack has meant "loose" and is a noun meaning "coal dust."

CHAPTER 16

DRIVE ME UP A WALL

MEANING
To be annoyed and/or very agitated.

HOW IT CAME TO BE

Do you enjoy fairy tales such as *Goldilocks and the Three Bears and The Three Little Pigs*? If your parents read you to sleep, you likely heard these stories repeatedly. Today's children's literature still tells the same stories, but now it tells them from various views. For instance, you likely heard the "Three Little Pigs" from an anonymous slightly-biased narrator; today's children can hear the same tale from that perspective, the pigs' perspective, and the wolf's perspective. It is the same story, but by sharing it through different narrator's eyes, one hears the story from various points of view. I can assure you the Big, Bad Wolf is not nearly so bad when relating the events.

As you might suspect, the history story also varies based on who tells it. One historical fact is that people used to build walls around their cities. Did you know that The Great Wall of China began as a series of walls around individual cities? Only later, the cities eventually merged the walls into one unit. These walls led to the idiom "drive me up a wall."

City leaders might tell you they built walls around their cities to keep people out. After all, there were lots of nomadic tribes that would raid farming villages. However, the invention of walls not only enabled leaders to keep people out, but they could also keep people in.

Imagine that you are a prisoner in a locked room. The only way out of your jail cell is a window out of reach. To get out, you will have to climb the wall literally. People used to climb walls if they were bored or felt trapped.

Now, pretend you are in a room with a vicious dog without an exit. Your only choice is to back into the wall, probably calling "Good doggy" as it salivates menacingly. "To have one's back to the wall" is also an idiom in contemporary culture; this sixteenth-century idiom means to have no place to go. This saying is from the point of view of the trapped victim.

Most people will not give up just because they have their back to the wall; they will look for a way to scale it and get out of the dog's way. Needless to say, when one feels that one must climb a wall, one is experiencing a circumstance that is very annoying and very agitating. "To climb the wall" means being driven to do things one would not ordinarily do. The dog requires you to climb the wall to survive; you have no choice if you want to live. If someone is making you climb the wall, you perceive that you have no choice but to tolerate what they are doing, although what they are doing is getting on your nerves. The idiom "To climb the wall" has over a 3,000-year history. Like "to have one's back to the wall", this is sharing the scene from the victim's perspective.

Now let's look at the situation from the aggressor's point of view. The dog has successfully herded you up the wall; it has driven you up the wall, just as a sheepdog drives sheep into the pasture. Believe it or not, "to drive someone up the wall" has nothing to do with cars. "To drive one up the wall" is a recent – 1950s – spinoff of "to climb the wall."

The idiom "to drive up the wall" is used increasingly in pop culture and has even been adapted by stairlift companies, manufacturers who make a pulley system for the elderly to sit in a chair and go up and down a wall. These ads keep the idiom fresh, and by keeping it fresh, they, in turn, keep their product on people's minds. Maybe those ads will "drive us up a wall!"

FUN FACTS

Rock climbing and wall climbing have been done of necessity since prehistoric times, but in the late 1800s people began climbing for sport. Britain's W. P. Haskett Smith is considered the father of the sport, for he started the fad by climbing Napes Needle in 1886.

The walls of the Great Wall of China stand about three times as high as an average height person.

During the Cold War, the Russians and East Germans built The Berlin Wall, a 96-mile wall around Berlin, Germany, separating East Germany from West Germany.

CHAPTER 17

FELL OFF THE WAGON

MEANING
To go back to old ways of thinking or living.

HOW IT CAME TO BE

Have you ever been on a hayride? You can relate to a wagon being pulled along the road slowly but steadily if you have. The wagon takes bumps hard, and it is possible to be jostled off if one is sitting near the edge or does not have a good sense of balance; that's why parents tell their small children to stay in the center of the wagon and away from the edges. The temptation to jump off the wagon and try to jump back on is always there, though, and you may even have seen people – especially teenagers - jump off the wagon so that they can run and jump back on. (The chaperones also tell the youth not to do it, but it seems somebody always does it anyway.).

If you have ridden on such a wagon, you can relate to what everyday mass transportation provided by churches was like at the beginning of the twentieth century. Instead of a gas-powered tractor, though, the wagon was pulled by horses.

At the beginning of the twentieth century, the Industrial Revolution had drawn many people to the city to seek their fortunes. However, these dreams did not always work out. Many of these fortune-seekers became prisoners of factory owners, barely eking out a living and never making enough to leave their position. Trapped, many turned to alcohol and lived on the streets. Many churches, particularly the newly founded Salvation Army, ministered to the poor, downtrodden, and neglected. They would pick up anyone who wanted a hot meal – the catch was the rider had to listen to a sermon before they could eat.

The years 1870 – 1910 were the height of the Social Gospel Movement, a time that saw churches focus on social issues. Realizing that many urbanites were so poor that they did not have transportation and lived so far from the church they could not walk, churches sent out wagons to bring people to church. Also, many children were factory employees, and since the factory was closed on Sundays, they had nothing to do all day but get in trouble. The Sunday School Movement intended to educate children and keep them off the streets.

The wagons were full of children, sinners, and saints. The churches were proud of the people they had reformed, and former alcoholics were paraded on the wagons. Sometimes, a marching band rode on or in front of the wagon. A former alcoholic or even an alcoholic on the way to the church was "on the wagon," committing themselves to a booze-free life.

Once in a while, though, a former alcoholic would return to drinking. He was usually ashamed of this and would try to hide it, but he would fall off the wagon - literally. Falling off the wagon quickly meant returning to one's old thinking.

Today, many people "hop on the bandwagon," whether for a political candidate, a popular cause, or a fad. When one loses interest, one is "off the wagon."

FUN FACTS

The Eighteenth Amendment declared most alcohol manufacturing, selling, and transporting illegal in the United States beginning in 1919; the Twenty-First Amendment in 1933 made them legal again.

To be a wagon, a vehicle must have four wheels; a cart must have two.

The wagon driver was often known as a "wagoner" or "teamster".

CHAPTER 18

FLIPPING THE BIRD

MEANING

To raise one's middle finger as a gesture of disgust.

HOW IT CAME TO BE

The raised middle finger is likely the oldest obscene gesture in Western society. It was first mentioned in the 423 B.C. play, The Clouds, by Aristophanes, a Greek playwright, but it was already well-known in culture then. To the Greeks, and possibly even prehistoric people, the raised middle finger was meant to represent the erect male penis with its testicles on either side and intended to show disgust at the speaker.

The gesture continues to be used throughout Western culture today. Just as in ancient days, it intends to convey disgust. It can be given in anger or playful banter. The gesture has several names, including "the one-finger salute," "giving the finger," "flipping someone off," and "giving someone the bird."

The first three names are likely self-explanatory. Just as soldiers salute out of respect when an officer of higher rank walks in, the person raising the middle finger in a "one-finger salute" is a mocking sign of respect. Since a particular finger is raised, "giving the finger" makes sense. Meanwhile, our middle finger often runs across our thumb; if we run it downward, we are "snapping"; if we run it upward, we are "flipping." Therefore, "flipping someone" makes sense as well. But what about "flipping the bird"?

We have covered "flipping," which is the upward raising of the finger. But where did the concept of "bird" come from? Was it just because the finger was taking flight? No, it is deeper than that.

The gesture began to be called "flipping the bird" in the 1940s because of its association with traveling vaudeville shows. Just like a thumbs down is given for something done poorly today, people would raise their middle finger if they were not happy with what they were watching. They would also boo and hiss. The hissing sounded like a goose. The finger and the goose were quickly associated with one another, and raising the middle finger became known as "flipping the bird."

The goose has been influential in other idioms as well. Perhaps you have heard of "cooking your goose", "goose bumps", "wild goose chase, "the goose that laid the golden egg," "what's good for the goose is good for the gander", and "silly goose". I hope you have enjoyed the history of "the bird" and haven't found it to be too loosey-goosey.

FUN FACTS

In Great Britain, the middle finger is often joined by the index finger to make a V, also called "flipping the bird."

Different people have different rituals for making the bird. Some just flip their middle fingers, but those with time may blow on the side of their fist while slowly raising their middle finger.

Usually, only one hand is used to flip the bird, but if a person simultaneously creates the gesture on each hand, it is called a "double bird."

CHAPTER 19

GET UP ON THE WRONG SIDE OF BED

MEANING
To be in a bad mood.

HOW IT CAME TO BE

Most of us are creatures of habit. Think about your morning routine. Chances are that you go through roughly the same motions every morning, and should you miss something, your day is upset. If I were guessing, even doing something a little nonroutine, such as getting out of the bed on the side you do not normally get out of, would feel weird. We have conditioned ourselves to believe there is a right side of the bed to rise from and a wrong side.

You are probably not even fully aware of your routine. For instance, you likely put the same foot down first every morning, but if I were to ask you which you put down, you would likely answer that you don't know. We are creatures of habit.

They believed that a person should always get up on the right side of the bed. It was a slight pun, for the right side was the right (non-left) side, as in the correct side. In ancient Rome, to do something with the left hand or left foot was considered evil, or at least second-rate compared with doing it with the right hand or right foot. Therefore, Romans always got up on the right side of the bed.

Caesar himself believed in this superstition. To prevent getting up on the wrong side of the bed, he put the left side of his bed against the wall.

The superstition likely came from the fact that most religions in the area prayed facing the East, the rising sun. If one faced East, the left hand faced North, the direction of the underworld. The left became associated with evil, and the right became associated with good.

Bad luck, of course, would put one in a foul mood. Over time, people in a foul mood in the morning were accused of waking up on the wrong side of the bed, even if they got out on the right side.

FUN FACTS

Researchers surveyed people on which side of the bed they got up on and what kind of mood they were in; according to the Independent, people who get out on the left side are significantly happier when they wake up than people who get up on the right side – just the opposite of what the idiom suggests.

Psychologists have found that one's mood often predicts how one's day will go; those who wake up in a bad mood are likely to have a miserable day.

In Christian cemeteries today, many people want to be buried facing the East because tradition says Christ will return from the East. The rising sun suggests resurrection both in its actions and in its pronunciation. In terms of action, the rising sun appears to be reborn in the east, whereas the sun appeared to have died when it set in the west the night before. In terms of pronunciation, the words "rising sun" reminds most Christians of the resurrected Jesus, the "rising Son."

CHAPTER 20

GLASS CEILING

MEANING
An invisible barrier that prevents one from advancing in an organization.

HOW IT CAME TO BE

Fishbowls and aquariums are common decorations in many homes and offices. People find looking at the fish to be relaxing. Do you have a fish tank where you are? If you do, go over to it and watch the fish for a few minutes before reading further.

A glass fish bowl holds water and allows you to see what is inside the bowl, much like having x-ray vision. You can see every twist and turn the fish makes – and the fish can see you. You can't touch the fish or go into its habitat because of the glass wall, but you can see it and imagine yourself in its environment. You can clearly see every detail of its environment, but you can not be a part of it because of the glass.

Now, look up. What do you see? You may see a ceiling, rafters, and a roof if you are indoors. You may even see a skylight. Imagine if that roof was made of glass, just like the fishbowl. You could see what is happening above you, but there would be no way to be a part of it because of the glass ceiling separating you from that environment.

This invisible see-through wall is what is meant by the idiom "glass ceiling." The metaphor "glass ceiling" was first used in 1978 by Marilyn Loden at the 1978 Women's Exposition in New York City as part of her Women's Rights Movement conference presentation. In those days, women working for corporations could watch the men around them get promoted, but they themselves could not rise to the top of most organizations; it was as if an invisible barrier prevented them from getting to where they wanted to be. Although women comprised almost half of the workforce, only 10% were chief executive officers at that time. The "glass ceiling" idiom has caught on with culture, but research shows that women are still underrepresented in the workforce's top positions. The term "glass ceiling" was originally intended to reflect a prejudice toward women. Still, over the years, it has come to mean prejudice against any under-represented minority group, with many members in lower positions but few, if any, in top positions.

FUN FACTS

The most famous ceiling is likely the Sistine Chapel, painted by Michelangelo, in Vatican City.

Clear glass is made from sand, soda ash, and lime.

To get colored glass, various minerals are added to the clear glass mixture. For instance, gold salts are added to make cranberry-red glass.

You may not have realized it, but you have likely seen something go 3,000 miles per hour; that is how fast a crack travels along a piece of glass.

CHAPTER 21

GO BERSERK

MEANING
To get violent, angry, and/or crazy, seemingly losing self-control.

HOW IT CAME TO BE

Every culture has heroes, and, over time, stories and legends are created about these heroes; these stories likely are not true, but they are still passed from generation to generation. Here in the United States, we have stories of George Washington, the great Revolutionary War general and the first President. If you believe the myths, he could throw a silver dollar coin from one side of the Potomac River to the other, a distance of over a mile. He was also responsible for chopping down a cherry tree and, when confronted with his chopping actions, supposedly said he could not tell a lie. Also, who hasn't heard that he had wooden teeth? Much of the details in these stories are not true.

People from other lands also have their heroes, and, just like our heroes, there are stories about them that may have some truth but should not be believed in total. For instance, the Norse tell stories of Berserk. Berserk was a warrior fiercely loyal to the god he worshiped, Odin, the supreme Norse god. The term "Berserk" means "bear skin," and since that is all that Berserk wore into battle, Berserk may not have been this warrior's true name; it may have been a nickname.

According to the legend, Berserk began his career as an ordinary warrior who wore armor like other warriors. However, one day while in the woods before a battle, he came across hallucinogenic mushrooms. Thinking the mushrooms were edible, ordinary mushrooms, he ate them. These were not ordinary mushrooms, however. These mushrooms made him think he was invisible, and they gave him the courage to do things no sane, order-following soldier would do. That day, Berserk painted himself blue and ran up to the enemy soldiers, disregarding his life. Berserk was the first person to truly "go Berserk."

He soon had followers who dressed exactly like him and behaved similarly. He formed a cult of followers he trained and who enjoyed the same nutrition. These Berserkers became feared for their brutality and disregard for cultural norms. They painted their bodies blue and wore no armor; they were unstable, uncontrollable, and unrepentant.

Undoubtedly, the Berserkers were real; they became mercenary soldiers for first-century kings. They were typically on the front lines, and because of their stark blue bodies and reputation of being more animal than human, they struck fear in their enemies. Like George Washington has been fictionalized, the Berserkers were also fictionalized and have even been associated with werewolves. You can't believe everything you read about them and their exploits. However, there is no doubt that the Berserkers were violent and unpredictable. Today, when somebody "goes Berserk," they share those traits. If somebody made you quit reading this book, would you go Berserk?

FUN FACTS

Berserkers lived in harsh conditions to toughen themselves.

Among the animals, Berserkers drew inspiration from were bears, hogs, and wolves.

The myth says that the Berserkers were shapeshifters and could become the animal they sought to imitate.

GOING TO FIND MYSELF

MEANING
Search for and/or find one's true character and talents.

HOW IT CAME TO BE

Ever misplaced something and have to go on a hunt to find it? How did you organize this "finding?" Did you try to recall the last time you saw it and then retrace your steps? Did you ask other people if they had seen it? Did you dump your pockets, look in purses, bookbags, briefcases, and backpacks, and check the area around you? People have different strategies for finding lost objects, and many incorporate all the strategies mentioned.

Just as we have been on quests to find objects, many people are on a quest to "find themselves." Ironically, all they have to do is look down, and there they are; they can also look in a mirror. Wherever they go, their body goes with them. This raises the question, "What does one mean when one is going to find oneself?"

"Finding oneself" is an inward journey to discover what one thinks, believes, and feels. It is a time of discovering new talents and personal growth. All these skills and beliefs were within the person, but the person had never taken time to pause to realize them before.

Finding oneself may sound selfish, but it doesn't have to be. In many cases, once one realizes one's talents, one can use them for the good of all of those around one.

To find oneself means looking carefully at one's past, particularly when the past had a life-changing choice, just as an automobile driver must choose which road to follow when a road forks. It also means comparing and contrasting oneself to those around one – parents, siblings, friends, and coworkers. Everyone is different, and being comfortable with those differences is important. It also involves thinking about one's goals. Many people allow life to push them as a roaring river moves a boat, but with goals, one can choose to sail to the place of one's own choosing. "Finding oneself" means looking at one's strengths and weaknesses, deciding how to use those strengths to get ahead, and overcoming any major weakness that could hold one back. Life has different meanings for different people – some people like possessions, some like friends, some value fame, some want to help others, some want to focus on the spiritual – and finding that meaning and making one's goal brings peace. Finding oneself means becoming who one is, not what others want one to be.

The concept of finding oneself likely originated in ancient Greece; the Greeks were the first culture to have luxury time people could use to contemplate. In Prometheus Bound, the playwright Aeschylus said to "know thyself." Socrates, meanwhile, suggested, "To find yourself, think for yourself."

It is easy to get busy with day-to-day routines and not go "finding ourselves." In most cases, we haven't lost ourselves, but we have not found our full potential. Finding ourselves can be a life-long adventure; one will not "find oneself" completely over a few days. The search for self, though, can be one of the greatest quests you ever undertake, even as great as learning about idioms.

FUN FACTS

When reflecting, you may find a strong urge to go into a particular field; this sense of direction is referred to as a "calling."

People sometimes experience paradigm shifts; when a paradigm shift happens, events that seem important may not be so anymore, and those that seem trivial may become important.

Psychologists such as those who created the Johari Window believe that one will never know everything about oneself, but they encourage everyone to find out as much as possible. The researchers said there are aspects of yourself that both you and the public know, aspects just you know, aspects the public knows and you don't, and aspects neither you nor the public know about you.

I'M GOING TO GET OFF MY SOAPBOX

MEANING
I'm concluding an impassioned speech.

HOW IT CAME TO BE

When you are ready to make a speech, what do you do?

If you are like me, you walk up to the stage – and many times the stage is raised, requiring one to climb steps to get to it, go over to the podium, tap on the microphone and say, "Testing, one, two, three; testing, one, two, three," and, having received confirmation that everyone can hear, then begin to talk.

Did you realize that the microphone was not invented until 1928? If one wanted to be heard by a crowd before then, one had to speak loudly, and, ideally, one needed to stand above the crowd. Standing above the crowd enabled people to see the speaker and, more importantly, to read lips. (You read lips, too; if you don't believe me, think how upset you were when the audio slipped just a fraction from the video while watching your favorite television show.) Standing higher than anyone else also enabled one to be the focus of attention.

People stood on anything they could find. Many gave speeches from tree stumps; today, we still say "stump for a candidate" when someone passionately talks about a candidate, even if they are not standing on a tree stump. One item lying around most communities in the 1800s was a soapbox, a wooden crate in which soap had been packaged to be sold in bulk to the general store; the soapbox made a perfect platform to stand upon. People would use the soapbox crates to stand on to address a crowd about whatever they felt passionate about – salespeople would talk about their products; politicians would talk about their ideas; and preachers would share the gospel; people would literally get on their soapbox before making an impassioned speech!

The soapbox was easy to obtain and very portable. Just as you may have gone to the local fast food restaurant to ask for boxes for moving or an empty pickle bucket for gardening, people would go to the local general store and request the soapbox, something the merchant was likely to regard as trash. The soapbox was easy to transport, so when a speaker came to town, the speaker didn't have to hunt down a stump or a soapbox; the speaker could just remove one from one's carriage.

FUN FACTS

The recipe for soap was first written down around 2800 B.C.E. in Babylon.

Queen Elizabeth I was known for bathing far more than the average person. She bathed four times per month! (I kid you not. Both of those sentences are true.)

The idiom "Don't throw the baby out with the bath water" came about because in Elizabethan culture, the father bathed first in a tub of water, then the mother, and then the children in age order. By the time the baby got put into the water, it was filthy, and the two were equally dirty.

CHAPTER 24

IN THE NICK OF TIME

MEANING
At the very last possible moment or at the moment,
one was needed.

HOW IT CAME TO BE

Have you ever used tally marks to keep track of things? When I was in elementary school, the teacher had us put tally marks on paper, and when we would get to five, she would have us "tie them together" with a diagonal mark. We would then start another group of five tally marks.

When early civilizations began to count, they likely used their fingers. Some cultures used their fingers and thumbs, and they count like we do, starting over with one when they reached a group of ten. Counting to ten in primitive cultures was easy, but people ran out of fingers and toes in cases where there was a lot to count, so they developed a tally mark system. (Other cultures, such as the Babylonians, used their fingers for counting, but they used just the four fingers on each hand. Each of the four fingers had three parts, so they created a base 12 system – which is what our clocks are on – instead of a base ten system.)

Tally marks heavily influenced the development of Roman numerals. In fact, to this day, the Roman numeral one is one tally mark, the numeral two is two tally marks, and the numeral three is three tally marks. Many clockmakers use four tally marks for the numeral four, although "IV" is the standard way. (Those who favor the nonstandard "IIII" claim they use it because many people do not understand that IV means "five minus one.") Tally marks also influence our numerals; for instance, it is more than a coincidence that our numeral one looks like a single tally mark. Each of those tally marks used by ancient counters was called a "nick." A nick was a razor-thin line that was placed on a stick.

Although the nick has been around since civilization, people did not use the nick as a way to express measurement until 1640. That tiny bit of difference, a nick, made all of the difference when someone says that the hero arrived "in the nick of time."

With the onset of the Industrial Revolution, things had to be precise. Precision became a necessity. Everything in society became more and more precise, and the amount of error that was acceptable declined. Factory owners didn't want too much inventory but needed enough raw goods for their workers. People were expected to be on the job at a particular moment, such as 8 a.m. sharp. Whereas the rising of the sun and the availability of rain dictated the activities of most of early civilization, now the clock and calendar were dictating what to do and when to do it. Precision – down to the size of a nick – mattered, so people began to talk about "the nick of time."

FUN FACTS

Before the invention of the calculator, people used to have nick sticks and long pieces of wood to keep track of sports scoring, inventory, and business deals.

To place a nick "scored" the wood, so those who keep track of nicks at sporting events became known as scorekeepers.

Many people use nicks as benchmarks today; someone in your family probably puts a "nick" on the chart or wall to show their child's height at different ages.

CHAPTER 25

IN THE TRENCHES

MEANING

Working on the front line where low-level employees engage the customer, a volatile, difficult, and demanding place where fast-thinking skills are needed, the action is tense, and theory is often replaced by pragmatism.

HOW IT CAME TO BE

Have you ever noticed that people stand approximately four feet apart when speaking to one another? If they are more than four feet apart, someone will step closer; if they are less than four feet, someone will step back.

Some people have trouble understanding these societal boundaries, so sometimes a no man's land is placed between individuals to clarify these boundaries. For instance, the convenience store has a counter approximately four feet between the customer and the cashier.

If you have ever stood behind a counter, you'll remember that the customer is in front of you and the wall is behind you. You are basically standing in a trench. If you don't want someone to notice you, you will duck behind the counter like a soldier would duck down into a trench in wartime when an enemy soldier gets too close.

In the back office of that convenience store is the manager. The manager, the store's general, does not get involved in day-to-day customer activities, just as modern generals are protected by the troops in the trenches. If the store gets busy, the manager must come out to assist; that is, the manager must get into the trenches.

"In the trenches" has a military background. During World War One in Europe, the Axis and the Allies had fought to a stalemate. Both had dug trenches along the Western Front, and anyone who tried to cross the small span of land between the two opposing trenches usually met death. The trenches were dangerous, for raising one's head to look out could get one killed; there was always the chance the other side would try to rush a group of soldiers to take the trench. Today, anybody "in the trenches" shares many characteristics displayed by the soldiers who lived and worked in these trenches.

FUN FACTS

The words "ditch" and "trench" can be used interchangeably, but usually, a ditch is shallower and constructed for irrigation.

World War One trenches were not straight lines; they were zig-zag. This zig-zag pattern prevented an enemy from firing down a straight line should an enemy get into the trench; the zig-zagging also helped stop shrapnel.

The trenches in World War I were hundreds of miles long. In most cases, on both sides, there was a trench on the front lines, a secondary trench line behind it, and a third line where headquarters were kept.

The trenches were a deadly place to be in World War One. One in ten soldiers died in the trenches from enemy fire or disease.

IT'S RAINING CATS AND DOGS

MEANING
It's raining heavily.

HOW IT CAME TO BE

Pause for a minute and come up with as many forms of rain as you can . . . and then resume reading.

Here are some words for rain: mist, light precipitation, sprinkle, mizzle, drizzle, thunderstorm, torrent, shower, deluge, and drops.

Although all these are terms for rain, they each describe a slightly different level of how much rain is falling and how fast it is falling. Even with all these words, though, sometimes words alone can't describe rain. How would one describe a really violent outpouring of heavy rain and winds? (If you can't do it, don't feel bad; neither could the originator of the idiom "It's raining cats an dogs." Although he couldn't find an English word to describe the violent storm, he could help his listeners grasp just how noisy and violent a particular storm in the late 1500s was by encouraging his listeners to recall how fast cats and dogs spun around fighting.

He was speaking figuratively; he was using a metaphor. However, the idiom caught on quickly because the literally-minded also considered it a good description. Many cats and dogs got swept up by rising currents, so seeing stray cats and dogs roaming the neighborhood after a horrific storm was a common sight.

Unless one thinks of the sound of the storm, this idiom may not make much sense. However, this idiom has retained its place in culture because children pass jokes from one generation to the next:

Beth: It's raining cats and dogs outside.
Breanna: I know. I just stepped in a poodle (puddle).

Country Carl: What's worse than it raining cats and dogs?
City Sally: Hailing taxies.

Dirk: It's raining cats and dogs outside.
Derrick: It's ruff weather that we are having.

Children may not fully understand what "raining cats and dogs" means, but they can't help giggling at the silly images the jokes bring to mind.

FUN FACTS

Raindrops can fall at a speed of 18 miles per hour.

The typical raindrop has a diameter of less than a quarter of an inch.

Although it rains water (and sometimes water and acid in the case of acid rain) on Earth, it rains things other than water on some other planets. For instance, on Venus, it rains sulfuric acid and methane.

JOSHING ME

MEANING
You must be joking.

HOW IT CAME TO BE

How is your fight or flight reflex? We all have the reflex. If we walk down a dark alley and a person steps out of the shadows, we have a built-in survival instinct – we will either seek to hold our ground or run away. We don't have all the details to be able to make a thought-out decision, but we must make a decision immediately. This requires making assumptions.

Want to admit it or not, we make assumptions throughout the day. We are often in a hurry and don't have time to look at all the details. We look over a situation, get general details, and let our minds assume the details we did not see. Josh Tatum realized that humans do this, and he made a small fortune by taking advantage of it.

Josh was a deaf-mute living in Boston in 1883 when the United States Mint released a new nickel. Josh noticed the nickel was roughly the size of the five-dollar gold coin in circulation. He had a couple of friends gold plate 1000 of the nickels, and then he went to bars and other dark places. He would attempt to purchase a cheap item, such as a cigar, and lay the plated nickel on the counter. The person behind the counter assumed it was a $5 gold piece and would give Josh the $4.95 change. Josh, of course, didn't tell the cashier about the mistake.

Josh was so successful that he had more nickels made. He worked his way from Boston to New York, giving his nickels in exchange for $4.95. Finally, in New York, he was caught. By then, he had made around $15,000; that's $40,000 in today's economy. The businesses he scammed took him to court – and he was found innocent. The judge noted that he had never told anyone the nickels weren't nickels, and therefore he had not lied. People had made assumptions, and Josh had taken advantage.

People still make assumptions; when they believe they are being led astray, the wise ones ask questions. When they ask, "Are you joshing me?" They are paying tribute to Josh Tatum. When the expression, "Are you joshing me?" first began, the "J" in "Josh" would have been capitalized because it was referring to a particular person. Over time, though, the idiom has gotten so common that it is no longer capitalized.

FUN FACTS

"Joshing" is an example of an eponym, a person's name which has become a verb because of what the person did.

The 1883 nickel, released in February, was revised by the U.S. government later that summer because of what Josh did.

Please don't follow in Josh's footsteps; while it was not illegal in his day, gold-plating or otherwise defacing money is now a federal crime.

CHAPTER 28

KNOCK ON WOOD

MEANING
Good luck.

HOW IT CAME TO BE

Did you grow up with an annoying sibling who was always spying on you and trying to listen to your private conversations? I did. If I was going to tell a secret to a friend or tell my mother something in confidence, I always had to ensure my sister was not hiding behind a chair or elsewhere in the room.

If you had a nosey sibling, you can relate to people in the Middle Ages. In the Middle Ages, if people had secrets to share, they often went into the woods where no other people were. The people of the Middle Ages believed that evil spirits lived in the forest's trees – evil spirits who would seek to tell their secret or interfere with their plans, and so before they would say anything, they would knock on wood to scare away the spirits.

People today may not believe in evil spirits and fairies lurking everywhere seeking to steal secrets, but most of us realize that privacy is merely an illusion. In 1942 with the outbreak of World War II, the United States put up posters of a brick wall with ears; the poster read, "Warning! Walls have ears. Be careful what you say!" The poster was a graphic attempt to urge people to be careful when they talk because other people might overhear them and steal their information. Today, Big Brother, a reference to George Orwell's 1984, is said to have cameras and microphones everywhere.

You can call me paranoid, but I don't trust my television, telephone, Alexa, and similar devices. When I want to tell a secret in my home, I often turn up the music. Just as the noise of the knocking would drown out the evil spirits' ability to hear, the noise of the music drowns out little sister's and Big Brother's attempts to eavesdrop.

In many cases, "knock on wood" today is used as an afterthought. Only after one has said something and does not want to jinx oneself does one add the afterthought, "knock on wood." For instance, "Math tests have been easy so far. Knock on wood." In many cases, the person may literally knock on wood just as ancestors of long ago would have, hoping to confuse the evil spirit so it does not comprehend and remember what it heard. Most people don't know why they say or do it, but they do know that it seems to help prevent chaos, so they carry on the tradition.

FUN FACTS

Some say, "Touch wood" instead of "Knock on wood."

Although most people knock on literal wood, some will jokingly knock on the forehead of the person they are talking to upon saying "knock on wood." This is especially true if the person has just revealed good news, said "Knock on wood," and is preparing to exit the room.

Although used interchangeably today, "touching wood" has different roots than "knock on wood." "Touching wood" may refer to the desire to touch the wooden cross Jesus was crucified on. Many people in the Middle Ages believed religious relics such as the cross of Jesus, the holy grail, and the bones of saints contained special powers within them, and touching them would bring good luck.

CHAPTER 29

LET THE CAT OUT OF THE BAG

MEANING
Let the secret be discovered.

HOW IT CAME TO BE

Have you ever gone shopping at a flea market, farmers' market, or grocery store? In many cases, the merchant who sells you the product will provide a bag so you can carry your purchase easier. Also, should you walk up to a similar merchant's table, you can look through their goods without being accused of stealing, provided you keep the bag closed.

Typically, the merchant will put the item in the bag, pull the bag tight, and then give the bag to the buyer. Most buyers don't check to ensure their merchandise is inside; they assume it is based on the weight and what they saw.

Some merchants, though, are not entirely honest. If the

buyer turns away momentarily, the merchant may substitute something in the bag for something else. For instance, if you purchased a rare music CD at the flea market, an unscrupulous merchant might replace the one you think you are purchasing with a different one and then resell the one you thought you bought. Such a swap almost happened to me at a flea market.It has happened more than once to me in the fast-food drive-thru – I am handed a folded sack, I judge it is correct by the weight and the fact the cashier said it is correct, and I leave; however, when I get home and empty the sack, I find that the cashier made substitutions I did not approve. Those swaps happen today, and they happened in the Middle Ages too.

In the Middle Ages, people would go to the market to buy piglets, hares, and other animals. The vendor would make the sale and put the animal in a bag. Unknown to the buyer, though, when the buyer was not looking, the vendor would swap the precious animal for a common cat. The bag's weight and movement were roughly the same, so the naive buyer had no idea. The bag was tied tightly so the animal could not get out while being transported and then handed with a smile to the buyer.

Once home, the shopper would open the bag, expecting to delight all around him with what he had bought. However, to his disgrace, the cat would jump out when he opened the bag. The cat was out of the bag; the secret that the man had been conned was now common knowledge.

FUN FACTS

To buy a "pig in a poke" is to buy something unseen; many people bought so-called piglets unseen only to discover they had bought a cat.

Scholars have found the phrase "let the cat out of the bag" in a letter the Protestant Reformer Martin Luther received on May 4, 1530. This may – or may not – have been its first use as an idiom.

Under medieval marketplace etiquette, should a buyer hear a "meow" or otherwise realize he had been duped, he had the right to return to the merchant to protest. Once the buyer made it home, though, the buyer had no recourse.

CHAPTER 30

MONEY LAUNDERING

MEANING
Making money gained illegally appear as
though it was legally gained.

HOW IT CAME TO BE

Does your family tell dad jokes?

Mine does. I often hear one when somebody leaves some coins or a dollar bill in their jeans, and the jeans go through the wash. The jokester will show off the soaked bill or shiny coin and say, "You better call the police. I just laundered money."

As a child, I took this joke as being a serious statement. After all, defacing money is a crime. Let me put your mind at ease, though, for I'm sure you are guilty of having washed a few coins, too – you aren't going to jail if you accidentally washed some money. Believe it or not, money laundering does have to do with laundromats.

Money laundering is an idiom for making illegally gained money appear to have been gained legally. The bank won't take money earned selling illegal drugs, engaging in prostitution, illegal gambling, human trafficking, or any other crime. It won't do it today and wouldn't do it in the days of Prohibition.

During Prohibition in the United States, 1920 – 1933, it was illegal to sell or transport alcohol. Those who dared to break the law were rewarded well financially if they weren't caught but couldn't spend their illegally gained cash. Therefore, people like the organized crime boss Al Capone bought all-cash businesses, such as laundries. He would then mix the illegally gained money into the money he claimed the laundry earned. For instance, if the laundry cleared $200, he might deposit $250; it wasn't enough for the bank to question because it could have all come from the laundry business.

When President Richard Nixon's advisors recalled how Al Capone had effectively hidden illegal cash, they used the term "money laundering." The advisors – and perhaps the President himself, wanted to find out the Democrats' plans for winning the 1972 election, so they decided to pay someone to bug the Democratic Party Headquarters in the Watergate Hotel in Washington, D.C. However, they didn't want the money to look like theirs. Therefore, they used a series of false fronts - The technical term for using a series of false fronts is "layering" – so the money couldn't be traced back to them.

The concept of layering goes back to at least China in 1-ish C.E. Chinese merchants didn't want civic authorities to know the various sources of where they earned their income, so they would hide the true source of it. It would be almost 1970 years before the act would be called "money laundering," but the act of money laundering is over 2000 years old.

FUN FACTS

Al Capone did jail time for tax evasion, not paying taxes on the money he claimed he earned legitimately, but he never did jail time for any other criminal act.

As Prohibition progressed and the mob made too much profit to be explained by laundromats and other small businesses, the mob's accountants shifted their illegally-obtained money to Swiss Bank Accounts.

Illegal money is considered "dirty," and legal money is considered "clean;" therefore, money laundering describes what happens to dirty money as it becomes integrated back into society.

CHAPTER 31

THE OLDEST TRICK IN THE BOOK

MEANING

It is a common ploy that everyone should know, and no one should fall for it; ironically, the idiom is often used after someone has fallen for the trick.

HOW IT CAME TO BE

The idiom, "You fell for the oldest trick in the book," is applied to any trick that is so common that people ideally should have sense enough not to let themselves get fooled by it. The concept of "trick" is fairly vague, and can apply to a magician's routine, a con artist's smooth talk, a prankster's attempt to make a fool of one, or a computer hacker finding ways to get computer owners to reveal passwords. Although the phrase, "You fell for the oldest trick in the book," is applied today to any trick that one should have known about, the questions arise, "What is THE oldest trick?" and "What book are we talking about?"

No one can say for sure what the earliest trick was, but a case can be made for what the earliest documented trick was. The earliest recorded magic tricks are found on cave walls in ancient Egypt, not a book. In a burial cave dating back over 4,000 years, archeologists have found drawings that indicate that the oldest trick may have been the shell game. The cave pictures cups being moved around on a flat surface. Scholars speculate the spectators were watching a cup with a ball in it as it was shuffled among the other two cups; when the trickster stopped shuffling, a representative from the audience was asked to choose which cup the ball was under. (Although this could be a game of skillful watching, the game is usually a con. The con is that the ball is lifted out of the cup during the shuffling, so, unknown to the audience, all three cups are empty.) That same painting also shows a second trick. Animals are being sawn into two pieces, similar to the cut-the-woman-in-half illusion magicians use today. Most people who see this trick know that magicians are humane enough not to cut a live woman in half, but they can't help believing the illusion the magician creates is real and that the animal/woman has been cut into two pieces. (Hint: the living animals' body parts were folded behind the animal and covered so no one looking head-on could see the so-called decapitated part.) Although it is generally accepted that this cave drawing is a painting of magicians entertaining the king, a minority of scholars say that this is a painting of servants preparing a feast for a king, the first group preparing beverages and the second preparing meats. Both tricks were included in the first book of tricks, what archeologists have called the Westcar Papyrus, around 1600 B.C.E.

Suppose these latter scholars are right about the burial cave painting being about chefs instead of magic tricks. In that case, the oldest magic trick recorded in history is the bowl that seemingly refills itself, a trick documented in ancient Greece. However, that just makes the refilling bowl the oldest magic trick; it did not appear in a book and therefore is not the oldest trick in the book. The ball-and-cup and saw-something-in-half tricks were put in the Westcar Papyrus; they may or may not be the oldest tricks, but one thing is for sure - they are the oldest to be recorded in the first book of tricks, making them the oldest tricks in the book.

FUN FACTS

Papyrus is regarded as the first form of paper.

In addition to being used as paper, papyrus was woven into sandals and baskets; it was even used to make boats.

Although papyrus was abundant in ancient Egypt, it is almost nonexistent in modern-day Egypt.

ON THE BALL

MEANING
Alert and prepared, able to adjust as the circumstances require.

HOW IT CAME TO BE

When you hear the phrase "on the ball," what kind of ball do you picture? Is it a tiny ball, like a marble; a small ball, like a baseball or tennis ball; a large ball, like a beach ball; or a giant ball, like an Earth ball? Is the ball round like a soccer ball, or is it oval like an American football? Is it wrapped in velvet like a tennis ball or made of rubber like a dodgeball?

When you are "on the ball," are you laying on it as if you snagged a fumble in American football, or are you standing on it, rolling it with your feet as a circus performer would?

If you are picturing yourself touching the ball in any way, you have the wrong picture of how this idiom came to be. "On the ball" is short for "keep your eyes on the ball," a saying that likely developed in rounders, the game that baseball is patterned after. When the other team batted, rounders had to be alert and ready for the ball to come to them. Today, adults still tell their children in Little League to "keep your eye on the ball," but the idiom has been shortened to merely "on the ball."

This is not to say that those people who don't know the idiom's history can't find a way to justify it by pointing out how a person could literally be on the ball, just as I had you try to do at the beginning of this section. These creative people point out how a soccer player has control of the ball when running with it, always being alert and prepared. The explanation works until one realizes that soccer was not around until the 1800s and cultural references to keeping on the ball were already in place.

FUN FACTS

Rounders began in England around 1485; it got its name because a person had to go 'round all four bases to score a point.

Rounders is still popular in England and Ireland today, although, just like American softball, it is a predominantly female sport today.

The phrase "on the ball" can be confusing in the ballpark. "Keep your eyes on the ball" is one of two "on the ball" sayings; "something on the ball" is another. In baseball, if there is "something on the ball," the pitcher has thrown the ball so that it will curve, sink, spin, and/or rise.

CHAPTER 33

ON THE FENCE

MEANING
To be undecided.

HOW IT CAME TO BE

Human beings are territorial. If you don't believe me, go to the grocery store, place a checkout divider down, and then wiggle your fingers over the airspace on the other side. You will be greeted by a hostile stare in most cases. People don't like other people in the space that they believe is theirs.

Rivers created the first property lines. Many towns, states, and countries still use rivers as their borders. When natural rivers were not available, people created moats. Moats weren't designed originally to keep people out; they were merely boundary markers. Moat-making was hard work, so people began to organize a fence line as a property line. The word fence comes from the word "defense," for the fence line showed wanderers what land the landowner was willing to defend. You have probably heard the idiom "Good fences make good neighbors," which means that if everybody respects the boundaries, all will be well; the fence itself is a no man's land, an area neither owns, and both share in the upkeep.

A person who is "on the fence" must decide which way to go – or perhaps not choosing a side is a real possibility. Politics is known for its "mudslinging", finding "dirt", errors, and weaknesses about the other candidate and then sharing that dirt with the public. In the early days, "being on the fence" meant having mud-free hands and feet, so the fence was sometimes the right place to be.

Today, "being on the fence" means to be undecided. Although sitting on the fence was considered a virtue and sometimes still is, in many cases today, it is said in disgust if one is accused of being on the fence. To a proponent who truly believes in a cause, the person unwilling to commit is more disgusting than the person who proclaims being for the other side. Advocates judge fence sitters as uninformed and/or apathetic, people that don't know and/or don't care.

FUN FACTS

The American poet Robert Frost helped popularize the idiom, "Good fences make good neighbors," with his poem *Mending Wall* in 1914.

Early fences were made of wood, bricks, mounds of earth, or mere hedge rows. Although some were for defense from invaders, most were mere boundary markers.

Barbed wire was not invented until 1874; Joseph Glidden invented it to maintain cattle.

OPENING A CAN OF WORMS

MEANING

An action that resolves one problem creates numerous other problems. Once these problems are created, they too must be faced; therefore, one may be better off not resolving the first problem proposed.

HOW IT CAME TO BE

Have you ever been fishing? If you have, you know that you have to put bait on the hook to attract the fish. People often use bread, flies, artificial bait, and . . . worms. Worms are popular bait because the worm will twist and wiggle, attracting the fish.

In rural America in the 1920s, fishing was no longer something most people had to do to survive; instead, it was a recreational activity that – thanks to the automobile, both city folk and rural folk could engage in on weekends. Many city folks didn't have the time or desire to dig their worms, so they would buy them pre-packaged in cans from bait stores.

Having the worms prepackaged in a can solved the problem of having to find bait, but little did the novice fisher realize by solving this one problem, numerous other problems would arise. The novice angler would open the can, put one worm on the hook, set the can aside, and then cast the line into the water. Life seemed perfect.

While the angler was engrossed in waiting for a fish's tug, the remaining worms were making their escape. One worm might tunnel into nearby earth, one might get into the fisher's coat on the ground, and another might burrow deeper into the can. When the fisherman realized there was a problem, the fisherman would try to regain control, but the odds of getting all the worms corralled again was almost nil.

Although the worms were in the can the whole time, they were no problem whatsoever until the can was opened. However, once the can was opened, the past was forever gone. Although the idiom "open a can of worms" likely has its roots in the 1920s, it became a common idiom when it made it into print in the 1950s when it was applied to U.S. President Dwight Eisenhower's political issues. From that time on, it has been common in American English.

Don't get the impression that bait shop owners were cruel, putting worms into steel cans with no air holes. The metal containers they used had air holes and also handles. The bait shop owners, in turn, received their worms from worm farms. Today, a "can of worms" is likely a plastic container or Styrofoam box of worms. These worms typically come from worm farms; they are not dug up willy-nilly on somebody's lawn.

The more I think about it, the more questions I have. Ironically, this question about a can of worms has opened a "can of worms."

A PIECE OF CAKE

MEANING
It's easy to do.

HOW IT CAME TO BE

I love desserts. If you offered me a choice of a vegetable or a dessert, I would almost always choose the dessert. It appeals to me whether it is cake, pie, ice cream, candy, cinnamon rolls, or cookies.

I am not alone. I suspect you would also prefer a chocolate cake to buttered broccoli, ice cream to celery, and cherry pie to chopped lettuce. Throughout history, people have loved all foods but seem to have loved dessert the most.

Getting down a piece of cake is not hard to do; getting down raw sushi might be another story. Because dessert is so easy to get down, if a task is easy, it is considered "a piece of cake." Although the saying "a piece of cake" found its way into both English and American society in the 1930s, the concept of cake being associated with easy dates back to Middle English, for even the playwright William Shakespeare used cake as a metaphor for something being easy.

"A piece of cake" refers to two aspects of easiness simultaneously. The first aspect is how hard the task is. If a task is a piece of cake, it is not hard. The second aspect is how much expertise is needed to complete the task. If the task is "a piece of cake," it can be handled by almost anyone.

"A piece of cake" is not the only idiom based on people's love for dessert. Somebody may also say, "It's as easy as pie." That, too, means that it is very easy. We also have idioms of food that describe difficult tasks. For instance, let's compare "a tall order" to "a piece of cake." A tall order is a lot of food dishes being brought to a table and will require a skillful, experienced server, whereas a "piece of cake" is something that a novice server could deliver. Most of us love to eat, and we love fun and easy tasks.

FUN FACTS

The first wedding cakes were pieces of bread.

"Dessert" is a French word meaning "clear the table."

During the Middle Ages, pies were filled with meats, not fruits.

In addition to being "a piece of cake" or "as easy as pie," if something is easy, it can be "as easy as 1, 2, 3" and "as easy as A, B, C."

CHAPTER 36

THE PROOF IS IN THE PUDDING

MEANING
The best way to see if something works is to test it.

HOW IT CAME TO BE

Do you like to mix your food together? I have seen people put together some very weird combinations. For instance, at a buffet, you can get potatoes, peas, cheese, spaghetti, potato chips, and meat sauce and mix them all together. My friend tells me it is delicious; I am not convinced. She has said that tasting it is the only way to find out.

Tasting something is not only a way to determine if something is yummy but also to determine if something is spoiled. I despise wasting money, so I will attempt to drink milk a day or two past its sell-by date. After just a sip, I can tell if the milk has started to go bad. In the Middle Ages, people tasted the food they were about to eat for both reasons.

In the Middle Ages, people did not have refrigerators, so a little bit of each food was put in a sausage-like sleeve and served at the meal's start. Whereas we think of pudding as a dessert, they called the concoction "pudding." If no one got sick or complained of a nasty taste, the food was considered good to eat, and the dinner party would commence.

Just like police have to have evidence to make an arrest, dinner guests had to have evidence that the food was bad before they refused to eat it. The police refer to their evidence as "proof," and the dinner guests did the same. Therefore, when they said that "the proof is in the pudding," they meant the evidence that the meal was not fit to eat was in the sample that had been served.

Today, we apply the idiom to more than food, but the concept of trying something before making a judgment remains the meaning behind the idiom.

FUN FACTS

Instead of saying, "Dinner time," when people were called to the table, the hostess would call, "Pudding time."

Because eating the pudding and discovering something was bad saved so many lives, "pudding time" came to mean what we mean when we say "in the nick of time" or "at the last second." Just as we no longer eat the pudding as our ancestors did, we no longer say "pudding time" for surviving a near-death experience.

"Pudding" is rooted in the French word for "small sausage."

THE RAT RACE

MEANING

A situation in which one perceives that one has no choice but to compete furiously with others for a predetermined reward such as money, power, and status.

HOW IT CAME TO BE

People race all kinds of animals. Horses and greyhounds are usually raced on tracks, much like the human Olympic running events. Slugs and turtles are also raced; usually, they are all placed in the center of a circle within a circle, and the winner is the first to cross out of the second circle. People even race rats!

If the contestants agree that the race is fair, any rules can govern a rat race. For instance, the contestants may each enter a maze one at a time and scurry around until the cheese is found.

Each rat is timed, and the one with the shortest time is declared the winner. Another version is to simultaneously have several rats at the starting point and see which reaches the end first.

Believe it or not, the term "rat race" did not describe the racing of mouse-like critters when it originated. The first rat race was done by pilots in the 1930s. The lead pilot would do loops and tight turns, and the other pilots had to follow. If you have ever sat quietly at night and watched as rats will follow a trail laid by other rats to avoid danger, then you understand why the pilots called the game "rat race."

When most people think of the "rat race," they don't think of pilots. As the term came into usage, the image people had shifted to the scene you were likely picturing earlier, a rat stuck in a maze with no way out trying frantically to find the cheese before some other rat could claim it.

Today, "rat race" is generally preceded by "the." There may be individual rat races in various cities, but there is only one for the human condition. The universal daily grind causes interstates to back up, people to act frantic, and a sense of hopelessness among the working class. Rats are notorious for hanging around filth and grime, and a "dirty rat" is a redundancy and an idiom; we are all like rats trying to survive in a hostile world. We didn't choose to be in the disgusting environment where we find ourselves, but now that we are there, we have no choice but to race to survive.

FUN FACTS

A rat's teeth are so strong it can chew through a cinder block.

Rats can move their left eye one way and the other the opposite.

When a rat is happy, its ears will droop.

Rats inhabit every continent except Antarctica.

CHAPTER 38

SKELETON IN THE CLOSET

MEANING
A secret you don't want anyone to know.

HOW IT CAME TO BE

What's in your bedroom closet? Purses? Jeans? A shelf for books? A dresser? Got any skeletons?

A closet is a place where guests are not welcome. When my parents knew company was coming and didn't have time to clean the house thoroughly, they would toss things into the closet. By the time the guests arrived, the living room looked very attractive, but unknown to the guests, the closet was a mess.

The closet has always been a place of privacy. It is an area the self knows but that is consciously closed off to the world. The idiom "to come out of the closet" or simply "come out" means showing the world who you are. The LGBTQA+ movement uses this idiom to refer to revealing one's sexuality/gender identity to friends and/or family, but all of us have things we don't share, even with those closest to us. We wear a figurative mask in society; we behave a certain way because we believe that is what is expected. As we get to know people more, we slowly remove that mask and reveal our true selves.

Along the same lines, most of us have a secret that most people in society would not understand or would reject us for, and therefore we keep it hidden. This secret is the "skeleton in the closet." The idiom is meant to remind us of a murder victim whom we have stashed and who, over time, has become merely bones.

Believe it or not, back in the 1700s, people had skeletons in their closets – and most of these skeleton hiders were not murderers. That's right; people stored human remains in their closets. It was illegal, but that didn't deter the researchers. These skeleton-hiders were scientists who wanted to study the human body in detail, so they hid their research specimens. Most of these skeletons were not murder victims – they were victims of grave robbers, public hangings, and bodies that had washed on shore with the tide. (Believe it or not, people found a secret room in Benjamin Franklin's London house where his roommate kept dead bodies.)

One's closet is always close to family and friends; anyone could open it anytime. The idiom, then, conveys a sense of immediate danger. One must always be on guard, or one's secret will be exposed.

Having a skeleton in your closet can ruin your life; just ask preachers and politicians who have had extramarital affairs, made shady deals, or don't follow their own advice. If at all possible, make your skeleton common knowledge. If you are the one who reveals it, you can favorably spin the story; you also ensure that no one can blackmail you or use it against you.

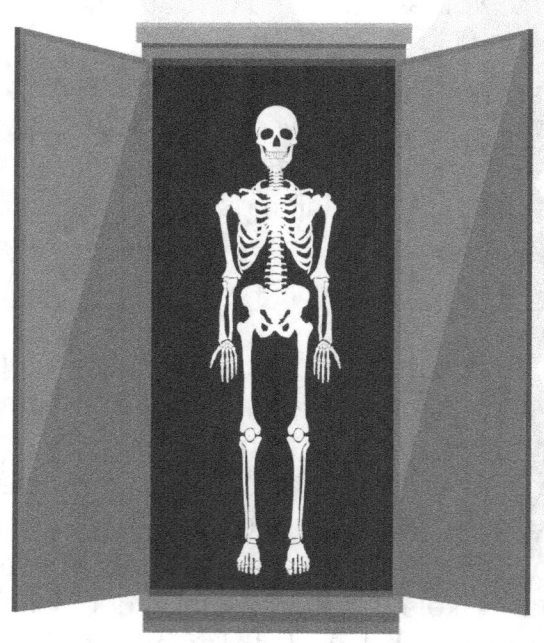

FUN FACTS

Although the idiom "skeleton in your closet" originated in England in the 1800s, today in England, the term closet is associated with "the water closet," the restroom.

The average human has 206 bones; some have more or less, based on how the bones have fused.

Providing dead bodies to researchers in the 1700s could be a full-time, well-paying job.

SPILL THE BEANS

MEANING
To share the truth.

HOW IT CAME TO BE

Have you ever been to a polling station at election time? If you have, you have seen voting booths and cubicles that people go behind so they can vote. The cubicles allow people to vote in private; no one is allowed to watch them vote. This secrecy enables them to vote their conscience without fear of retaliation.

Recently, people were given a paper ballot and punched holes in it. The ballot was then placed like a coin in a piggy bank into a ballot box. At the end of the day, the ballots were run through a computer, and a computer would then count the punches.

Voting one's conscience is not only a right in a democracy; it is the backbone of it. The concept of democracy dates back to ancient Greeks, people who voted long before the paper ballot originated. The Greeks had a ballot box, but instead of paper, which was not invented yet, they put beans into it. For instance, a white bean was a "yes," and a black bean was a "no."

Once in a while, someone knocked down the ballot box holding the beans, scattering the beans on the ground for all to see. People could look and see how the vote was progressing. Even worse, they could tell if people were lying to them; for instance, if everyone said they had voted with a white bean and the jar had a black bean, someone was lying.

Today, when we tell the truth about something that is supposed to be a secret, we are "spilling the beans." Although spilling "beans" is where the idiom began, today, people can also spill "it" or "their guts," and these expressions mean the same thing.

FUN FACTS

For major contracts to be awarded in ancient Greece, everybody on the committee had to approve the contract; that is, there had to be 100% white beans in the ballot box. The contractor had been "blackballed" if there was a black bean.

"You don't know beans" means one lacks common sense. It goes back to rural America in the 1800s. Farmers visiting the general store often asked out-of-towners questions about bean farming to determine if the visitor had a rural background; upon failing the quiz, the farmers would scoff, "You don't know beans!"

The first farmed beans were grown in Egypt over 5,000 years ago.

CHAPTER 40

STABBED IN THE BACK

MEANING
To have been betrayed by someone regarded as a friend.

HOW IT CAME TO BE

Have you ever experienced a "squeeze hug"? The squeeze hug is the most intimate of the 14 hugging styles. The person stands before you puts their arms around you, draws you close, and squeezes. You likely reciprocated, wrapping your arms around the hugger and squeezing back.

Most of the time, we don't let people within our personal space. Don't you believe me? Walk up to somebody at a restaurant and stand toe to toe with them; they are likely to take a step backward, walk away and call you a "freak," or push you back, possibly asking, "What's wrong with you?" In the United States and England, we typically stand about three feet apart from friends; any closer makes us uncomfortable.

For somebody to give you a squeeze hug, you must trust them. Now, imagine what you would feel if that person quietly slipped out a knife they had hidden up their sleeve and stabbed you in the back as hard as possible. Being stabbed in the back is a bitter betrayal, for you trusted that person more than anyone else.

Being stabbed in the back has happened both figuratively and literally throughout history. One of the most famous instances was the Ides of March, in which Brutus stabbed Julius Caesar. The instances may have been happening for thousands of years, but the idiom did not originate until the end of World War I. The German soldiers who were fighting in the war knew the cost of life and the damage the war had done, and they didn't want to walk away without having accomplished anything; however, the German politicians, fearing strikes and chaos on the home front, wanted to bring the war to a close, so when the politicians announced the war was over, the soldiers felt as if they had been stabbed in the back. The phrase became popular worldwide in 1919 when the German commander-in-chief was asked why the Germans lost; he did not believe the Germans had lost on the battlefield, so he quoted what he said he had heard an English general say, "We were stabbed in the back."

FUN FACTS

The shopkeepers who threatened to strike were not all Jewish. Still, Adolf Hitler used the threatened strikes by Jewish merchants to justify the Holocaust and to endear himself to the German military.

The amount of personal space one needs varies by culture; an American or English person will expect more personal space than a Japanese person.

The squeeze hug is the most romantic of the hugs, but other popular hugs include the side-by-side hug, the bear hug, and the one-sided, one-arm hug.

SWEET DREAMS

MEANING
A way to wish somebody a restful sleep.

HOW IT CAME TO BE

How much time per day do you spend sleeping? The average person sleeps between seven and nine hours in a twenty-four-hour period. Everyone needs sleep, regardless of race, gender, creed, income status, or political affiliation.

It is fitting that humans wish each other a restful sleep. One idiom that does this is "sweet dreams." Sleep researchers believe that a person dreams four to six dreams per night, which can be pleasant experiences or nightmares. The word "sweet" in this phrase does not refer to sugar but to an overall pleasant experience. By calling "sweet dreams," the speaker is not only calling out a wish but, more importantly, perhaps, the caller is putting one's mind in a positive frame.

Beds date back to the early days of farming when nomadic people ceased wandering and began setting up permanent residences and working the ground around them. The mattresses and bed frames we know today became common around 1700 when this saying occurred. The bed was a piece of home furniture, and ritual surrounded it.

In more recent times, "sweet dreams" has also come to mean one's goals in life and what makes one happy. In many cases, these goals are dreams; the reality is that they may never come true. However, they succeed in motivating one to continue to push for them.

In many cases, the quest is satisfying, even if the dream never fully comes to pass.

Some people rudely point out that these goals are just fantasies, saying the idiom, "In your dreams!" sarcastically to emphasize that it is just a dream. The retort to this is another idiom, "One can dream, can't he/she?" Ultimately, each person controls their mindset, and they can "dream up" whatever they want. Pardon another idiom, but if they want, they can "live in a dream world" if they choose to do so. With hard work, to many people's amazement, these sweet dreams can become sweet realities, for "dreams do come true," reality may even surpass and "go beyond your wildest dreams." Dare to dream!

FUN FACTS

When "sweet dreams" originated, people had mattresses made of wool, cotton, horsehair, and coconut fibers; Memory Foam, used in many mattresses today, was not invented until 1966.

Dreams last between 10 and 20 minutes.

Nightmares typically occur in the last third of one's sleep.

THAT'S ALL SHE WROTE

MEANING
It has come to a bitter end.

HOW IT CAME TO BE

Have you ever received a letter in the mail? Before the computer brought about email, sending letters by the postal service was an everyday way for people to keep in touch. It was common for a friend or relative to address a letter, especially a Christmas card, to the head of the household, knowing that the head of the household – almost aways a male at that time – would share the letter with the family. When the head of the household got a personalized letter, other people gathered around him, and he read it aloud. As the speaker finished reading the letter, he would announce, "That's all she wrote." "That's all she wrote" began as a literal expression for "there is nothing left to read."

During World War II, the phrase "that's all she wrote" became an American idiom and picked up a more depressing meaning. Soldiers fought overseas in Europe and the Pacific and occasionally received letters from family and friends – especially girlfriends. Very few such letters arrived in each day's mail call, so those lucky few soldiers who received a personalized letter were often surrounded by their friends who were curious about the contents. The soldier who received the letter from his girlfriend back home would open the envelope enthusiastically, perhaps even sniffing it for the trace of perfume his heartthrob wore. Amid the whoops and laughter as he read through the letter in front of everybody, sometimes a soldier would realize - to his horror - that it was a letter saying that she could not handle the long-distance relationship and/or that she had found somebody new. The soldier would bravely finish reading the letter in humiliation and then stammer, "That's all she wrote." Today, "that's all she wrote" doesn't just mean coming to an end; it means coming to a bitter, unexpectedly sad end.

A soldier getting dumped by his girlfriend back home was fairly common; the war tested the relationship. The letters were so common that soldiers began to refer to them as "Dear John" letters, and the "she" in "that's all she wrote" is not meant to pinpoint any particular woman.

The meaning of "that's all she wrote" goes even deeper than merely just being a bitter end; it is the end of a relationship, an era in one's life. It has become the conclusion of one stage that can never be revisited except through nostalgic memories and a new beginning. Whereas many people fight change, the speaker of "That's all she wrote" accepts the loss of the past, even though the loss is painful. Even though the speaker of "That's all she wrote" is sad, he is ready to let go of the past and go into the unknown future.

FUN FACTS

The first commercial Christmas card was drawn in 1843 in England. Idioms are often used in country music; in 1942, Earnest Tubb used the idiom "That's all she wrote" in a song appropriately named That's All She Wrote.

Mail to soldiers was often called V-mail, short for Victory Mail, because it was believed a letter from home inspired the soldier to remember who they were protecting in the war.

THE THIRD TIME'S A CHARM

MEANING
Keep trying, and eventually, you will get it done.

HOW IT CAME TO BE

Both England and the United States have Judeo-Christian roots. Our society has gotten more secular over the years, and many people no longer recognize the significance of the symbology that past generations placed upon numbers. If you have read Revelation and other Biblical texts, you have probably encountered small numbers like 3, 4, 5, 6, 7, and 10 and larger numbers like 666, 777, and 1,000. To understand why the third time was considered so special, let's review why the numeral three was so significant to our Judeo-Christian ancestors. Here is a quick review of numerical symbols.

3 – symbolizes the Father, Son, and Holy Spirit

4- the world; north, south, east, and west

5 – normal; the common person had five fingers per hand.

6 – an imposter; so close to both five and seven that it is easily mistaken

7 – the holy united with the earth; 3 + 4 = 7

10 – perfection; if you had ten fingers, you had perfect hands

666 – the most unholy number of all; three 6's

777 – the holiest number of all; three 7's

1000 – perfect perfection; 10 x 10 x 10

When you look at scriptures with this knowledge and at other writings, things begin to take a meaning very different than the literal meaning. (If you read Biblical commentaries, you will find that scholars sometimes disagree on when a number is meant to be taken literally and when it is meant to be taken symbolically.)

The idiom, "The third time's a charm," parallels the idiom, "Try, try, and try again." Both idioms advocate for at least three tries. So does the saying, "Testing, one, two, three," that speakers perform when doing a microphone check. The magic is in the perseverance, not the third attempt itself, so a fourth or fifth attempt might also be needed.

Although the symbolism of numbers goes back thousands of years, the idiom "The third time's a charm" only goes back to the 1800s. During the age in which European powers were sending voyages to colonize around the world, the idiom "the luck of the third adventure" had come into use, suggesting that just because an explorer had not found unknown lands on previous trips was no reason not to try another trip. That idiom became reworded as "the third time's a charm" and was applied to everyday life and exploring new lands.

The idiom gained wide usage thanks to John Lee and an English law that stated that one could not be hung more than three times. John was a thief accused of murdering his female employer in

1884; he was found guilty, although he vehemently denied killing her. He was scheduled to be hanged in February 1885, but after three failed attempts, the government had no choice but to show mercy and reduce his death sentence to life in prison. He was released in 1907 and began lecturing about his experience. He even became the subject of a silent movie. The third time was truly the charm for him.

FUN FACTS

Only one other besides John Lee, Joseph Samuel, has survived three public hanging attempts.

John Lee may not have been as lucky as he seemed. He may have had an accomplice who put a wedge in the hanging apparatus when it was operated and secretly removed it when it was inspected.

Recent studies have found that ten percent of Americans fear "13". Thirteen is traditionally unholy in Judeo-Christian society; a witches' coven must have exactly 13 members.

THROW IN THE TOWEL

MEANING
To quit.

HOW IT CAME TO BE

Have you bathed in the last few days? If you have, you likely used a towel to dry with. The first towel was created in Turkey about 400 years ago. The early Turkish towels served the same purposes as ours do, such as to wipe off sweat before a shower or to dry off after a bath, but, unlike most towels today, which are one solid color, early Turkish towels were works of art, having multiple colors and lots of embroidery.

The sport of boxing has been around since the early Greek Olympics. As with other sports, though, it has evolved. Boxing remained popular until the fall of the Roman Empire and then reemerged as a popular sport in the 1700s. At that time, a new tradition arose in boxing: the second, that person who stands in the boxer's corner and cheers, medicates, and coaches the boxer, began to throw the boxer's sponge into the ring if he believed that the boxer was not fit to continue. Sponges are small, though, and sometimes were not noticed by the referee; therefore, by 1900, throwing in the boxer's towel – a plain white towel -had become popular.

A white banner being a sign of surrender is nothing new. Chinese history shows a white banner was used in China in 25 C.E., and the Romans developed the idea by 106 A.D. Before the white flag was accepted as a sign of defeat, surrendering Roman armies would lift their shields to the sky. Even today, we tend to lift our hands when we want to surrender to somebody. The white banner was likely chosen not only because of how easily it could be seen but also because it showed neutrality, having a picture of neither warring party's flag on it.

The white towel symbolizes admitting defeat in boxing, but that has not always happened in war. Sometimes the stronger side will send representatives under a white flag to attempt to negotiate with their would-be opponent, giving the weaker side a chance to escape unharmed. Today, throwing in the towel means admitting defeat, not just in war or boxing, but in whatever one was doing.

FUN FACTS

Whereas "to throw in the towel" is an idiom meaning quitting, to "throw one's hat into the ring" means beginning.

There was an idiom, "throw in the sponge," before throwing in the towel became popular.

Not only can a boxing match be stopped by throwing in the towel, but a boxing match can also be stopped by a referee or knockout blow.

THROW UNDER THE BUS

MEANING
To sacrifice a friend for one's own security.

HOW IT CAME TO BE

Do you remember standing outside on cold winter mornings waiting for the school bus to come? If you live in an urban area, you have likely waited on a bus or subway in your adult life as well. At those bus stops, friends generally stand around and talk to one another. As the bus approaches, people form a line to prepare to board. Imagine, though, at the last second, if the person you thought was a friend pushed you in front of the bus. Pretty violent! And not very nice!

This is one of the newest idioms, barely 40 years old. It likely originated in England in the late 1970s but became part of American popular culture in 2008, when American political allies would suddenly switch loyalties from one candidate to another during the primary election process. Unlike most idioms, this idiom has not gelled yet in form, and you are likely to hear people say, "Throw her under a bus," "Push her in front of a bus," or "Throw her in front of the bus." The bottom line is the same – someone the victim thought was a friend is willing to let the victim take the blame for something, even if it means giving the victim up as a friend. No matter which version is used, if someone is accused of throwing someone under the bus, they are not doing the person they are throwing any favor.

The proverbial bus is usually a major event, such as a group report. Everybody in the group knows that the boss (or teacher if you are in school) will call on the group to present. After the presentation, the boss will find fault with the report, which is when a so-called teammate throws the victim under the bus. Before the 1980s, people were less urbanized and so a similar idiom, "throw you to the wolves," was used. In both cases, people are saving themselves by sacrificing you.

Everybody at the bus stop has the same goal – to get on the bus. The bus is going to take one to a grand destination. When one is "pushed under the bus," the bus runs one over, often destroying one's career. While the rest of the team may succeed in getting on the bus and safely reaching the destination, the person pushed under the bus will not be able to be a part of that success. Although some people may enjoy "being martyrs" and "taking a bullet for the boss," two idioms that express sacrificing oneself for a cause, people who are pushed in front of a bus usually are not sacrificing themselves by choice.

FUN FACTS

The word "bus" essentially means "transportation for all,"

The first bus line used horse-drawn carriages; it started in France in 1682.

The idiom "Throw under the bus" means to blame somebody else. At the opposite end of the spectrum, the idiom "The buck stops here" means to take full responsibility.

UPSET THE APPLE CART

MEANING
To ruin everything.

HOW IT CAME TO BE

Have you ever taken a deck of cards and made a house of cards? You can form walls by turning the cards on their sides and leaning them against each other. With skill, you can then add flooring and then add on another story. You can have several stories and a roof constructed of two cards forming a tower if you are talented. It doesn't take much to knock down a house of cards; frailty is suggested in the idiom a "house of cards."

Even though you realized it might not last, did you build such a house anyway? I have. And I have experienced somebody walking by, creating a breeze, and knocking the whole thing down.

Watching all that effort come crashing down made me frustrated, mad, and depressed simultaneously. (There is no English word to describe that feeling; that's why we have the idiom "upset the apple cart.") Have you had that feeling as well? If you have, you can relate to how an apple merchant feels when somebody knocks over his display.

The apple merchant has worked hard to stack the apples to appeal to prospective buyers. Not only are the apples displayed in a pyramid formation, but he has also worked to put the shiniest ones on display and turned the apples with bad spots so that the spots cannot be easily seen. The apple merchant has a plan, and when someone knocks over that display by rubbing against the cart or by taking a bottom apple, the whole plan falls apart. "To upset the apple cart" refers to the destruction of the plan.

The idiom dates back to the Roman Empire when it was simply "upset the cart." The "apple" part was added in 1788 by Jeremy Belknap in his History of New Hampshire, probably because the reading audience was in New Hampshire and apple carts were prevalent. The modified phrase caught on and is still used today.

FUN FACTS

Carts are at least 5,000 years old.

The surname "Cartwright" means someone in your family tree likely built carts; the surname Carter means someone in your family's history likely drove carts.

The apple symbolizes health, love, and fertility.

Apples are 25% air; this is why they float in water.

The average apple contains 80 calories.

CHAPTER 47

WEAR MANY HATS

MEANING
To have many different roles.

HOW IT CAME TO BE

Who are you? (Seriously, who are you? Take a minute and write down your answer. As you read this section, you will likely find that your writing reveals more about you than you realized you were sharing.)

We often hear the "Who are you?" question when we meet new people. When confronted with that question, most people identify by gender, family heritage, or occupation. Most people are all of this, plus more. Let's look at how you could have answered, and rest assured that the examples I give are by no means the only possible options.

- By citizenship. "I'm an American" or "I'm British."
- By gender. "I'm male" or "I'm female."
- By occupation. "I'm a student" or "I'm a construction worker."
- By political party. "I'm a Democrat" or "I'm a Republican."
- By family position. "I'm Rodney's son," "I'm Kelsey's father," or "I'm Suzanne's brother."
- By education level. "I'm a high school graduate" or "College student."
- By income level. "I'm a millionaire" or "I'm a welfare recipient."
- By religion. "I'm a Christian" or "I'm a Muslim."
- By race. "I'm an African American" or "I'm Oriental."
- By hobby. "I'm a golfer" or "I'm a photographer."
- By food preference. "I'm a vegan" or "I'm a meat eater."
- By birthplace. "I'm a Calhoun resident" or "I'm a Charlestonian."

The truth is everyone is many things simultaneously; you are something in each of those twelve categories. Although we use a phrase or two to describe ourselves, we are much more complex. We are many things to many different people. An idiom reflecting our diversity of us is "wear many hats." At school, we may wear our ballcap; at our fast-food job, we may wear a Burger Barn paper cap; and when outside playing with our friends in the snow, we may wear a stocking cap. Each cap reflects an aspect of our life, and yet no one hat captures our life completely.

In society, the hat we wear often determines how people perceive us; it also limits what we are supposed to say and do as we perform. I have seen people walk up to a stranger and give him their cell phone to look at just because he was wearing a cap that read "IT Pro." Many other youths the same age did not have the cap, and the man would never have offered them the phone. The hat conveyed that the youth was an IT professional. Most of us wear many hats, both figuratively and literally, and they all work together to form the person we call the self.

FUN FACTS

Bald men were likely the first people in human history to wear hats; they wore them to protect their exposed heads from the sun.

Hats likely began for practical reasons, such as to protect one from the sun and to keep one warm; later, they became fashion statements.

In 1571, England passed a law requiring every non-noble male over six to wear a hat on Sundays and holidays. The Cappers Act, as the law was called, was designed to stimulate the sale of wool.

CHAPTER 48

WHEN PIGS FLY

MEANING
It's not going to happen.

HOW IT CAME TO BE

Nothing in life is certain; likewise, nothing is impossible!

You may argue that "death and taxes" will always be there. If the rapture is real, you might be called to Heaven without dying. Taxes to the federal government aren't guaranteed either, for there is a slim chance that aliens could invade the country and taxes would no longer exist.

At the opposite extreme, nothing is impossible. In this crazy world, it is always possible that aliens will take over the White House. Is it likely to happen; no. But could it happen; we can't rule it out.

Words like "rare" are used for things that are not likely to happen; words like "almost always" are used for things that are likely to happen. These qualifiers provide wiggle room, allowing for an exception.

Several idioms have arisen to reflect that things are not likely to happen. "When Hell freezes over" is one. Hell is known as an eternal furnace, so it is not likely to happen. The other, the focus of this essay, is "when pigs fly."

Cows, horses, donkeys, and many other animals don't fly either. Pigs are the most grounded animals, known for rolling in the mud and becoming one with the earth. Pigs are also known for being big and fat, so while horses engage in equestrian activities such as jumping hurdles, pigs can't even get off the ground. The odds of pigs flying are very, very remote, far more remote than other animals.

In its infancy, the idiom, likely inspired by a Scottish poet, added a second phrase, "with their tail forward." In other words, the pig was not only flying, but it was able to fly backward and at a speed fast enough to lift the pig's tail into the air. "When pigs fly" has become a common expression and has led to other expressions. For instance, occasionally, when something rare happens, such as a traditionally pitiful team winning a championship, you may hear someone point at the success and exclaim, "A flying pig!"

FUN FACTS

Pigs regulate their body temperature by lying in the mud; they do not sweat.

Aside from humans, pigs are the smartest animals on earth. The typical pig has the intelligence quotient (IQ) of a human three-year-old.

Despite their reputation as dirty animals, pigs are among the cleanest. For instance, if given a chance, they relieve themselves far from where they live.

WHITE LIE

MEANING
An untruth told to amuse or build up a friend.

HOW IT CAME TO BE

Do you remember passing your driver's test? The written tests vary, but my copy had questions about road signs. The colors of road signs in the United States mean something; that way, if you have a particular need, you can look for a particular color as you drive. For instance, rest stops will be blue, so if you are searching for a rest stop, you know to be looking for a blue sign. In case you have forgotten, here is a quick review of the sign colors used by the Department of Transportation in the United States:

Red – danger; stop
Yellow – caution
Orange – construction
Green – go
Blue – guide

Brown – scenic spots
White - regulations

Colors have been symbolic for centuries. In addition to regulations, white is used in today's culture to signify purity, for white is untainted by any other color. For instance, most brides wear white, angels are often pictured frolicking in white gowns, and many doctors wear white lab coats.

A lie is the opposite of truth; therefore, one would expect it to be bad – and often, it is. However, in our society, we have "white lies," that is, pure lies, lies that have no evil in them. You might give this kind of lie when you don't want to hurt somebody's feelings. For instance, if your friend asks you if she looks good in her new dress and you don't think so, you may tell a "white lie" to not hurt her feelings. Another type of white lie is an exaggeration or a minimization, making something seem better or worse than it is. White lies told as exaggerations are often done so to make a story more entertaining. For instance, the senior adult may tell his grandson, "I walked over a mile to school each day," when, in fact, it was only three blocks.

Although people have likely been lying to each other since the beginning of time, the word "lie" did not become part of the English vocabulary until around 600 C.E. It was over 800 years more, around the year 1400, when the term "white lie" first appeared. The distinction between a common lie and a "white lie" is subjective; different people have different definitions. What one person accepts as a "white lie" another may consider an outright lie, so I advise avoiding lies of any type whenever possible.

FUN FACTS

People are prone to lie less in person than when they text or write.

Lying and keeping track of lies can create mental stress; researchers have found that people who tell the truth are generally much happier.

When a person thinks about lying, they often develop their creativity.

When people lie, they use a smaller vocabulary than normally, partly because their minds are busy trying to think of the lie.

CHAPTER 50

YOU'RE PULLING MY LEG

MEANING

If someone pulls your leg, the other person exaggerates the truth, trying to trick you into believing something untrue.

HOW IT CAME TO BE

I've got a confession to make – I have done some mean things in the past. For instance, back in grade school, I used to stick my foot into the aisle as the girl I had a crush on was returning to her seat, causing her to trip and drop whatever she was carrying. The people around me laughed – and I did have her undivided attention; that seemed to make it all right – but it really wasn't.

I didn't realize it, but I was literally pulling her leg with mine. I would catch her leg and hold it; she would pull her leg with her hips to go forward, but she fell flat on her face instead. Tripping somebody is a relatively harmless prank, and "to pull somebody's leg" has come to mean to make someone look foolish. Instead of tripping people – which can result in broken bones and other injuries, pranksters who "pull people's leg" exaggerate the truth to the naive listener, who will then appear foolish in front of everyone, repeating what he has heard.

The English language is always changing. Just as we in the past few years have seen a "text" go from being a book to being a message on the phone, the term. "To pull somebody's leg" has had other meanings throughout history. For instance, in the 1600s, it meant "to help, to ease one's pain." The current meaning of "pulling one's leg" came into being in the nineteenth century because of con artists and has been a part of popular culture in England and the United States since the early twentieth century.

Con artists - usually a ring leader and a crony - used to sit on a public park bench watching people walk by, waiting for a wealthy, unobserving victim to come along. When the wealthy person passed, the ring leader would trip the victim with either his leg or a cane, sending the unsuspecting wealthy victim flying to the ground. Very apologetically, the crook(s) would then help the victim up. The crook(s) would pickpocket the victim in all the commotion.

To the victim, everything that he had experienced was real, from the accidental tripping to the genuine care he had received. The con artists had pulled his leg literally, and "pulling one's leg" soon became a figurative expression. The concept of trying to trick someone into believing an experience to be true that wasn't true references this con.

FUN FACTS

Another "pull somebody's leg" con was when a con artist's assistant would come up hobbling to the medicine man/faith healer, claiming one leg was shorter than the other. The conman would then pull the shorter leg, making it the length of the other leg. This gave the conman credibility, and the gullible in the audience would believe the faith healer could cure them too.

The term "con man" is short for "confidence man," these people would gain their audience's confidence and trust before taking advantage of them.

Two other popular "leg" idioms are "to grow legs and walk away" and "don't have a leg to stand on." The first means to "disappear mysteriously," and the latter means "unable to prove something and win the debate."

To avoid sexist language, avoid the term "con man" and utilize "con artist."

REFERENCES

Introduction: What is an Idiom?
https://www.grammarly.com/blog/idiom/
https://www.phrases.org.uk/idioms/index.html
https://writingexplained.org/grammar-dictionary/idiom

Chapter One: Age Before Beauty
https://en.wikipedia.org/wiki/Courtesy_book
https://english.stackexchange.com/questions/48744/who-will-say-age-before-beauty-more-often-man-or-woman-young-or-old
https://idioms.thefreedictionary.com/age+before+beauty
https://wordhistories.net/2018/05/09/age-before-beauty/

Chapter Two: All Went South
https://english.stackexchange.com/questions/42358/origin-of-the-idiom-go-south https://ell.stackexchange.com/questions/13743/what-does-things-went-south-mean#
https://idioms.thefreedictionary.com/thing+go+south
https://idioms.thefreedictionary.com/thumbs+up ttps://idioms.thefreedictionary.com/went+south

Chapter Three: Back to the Drawing Board
https://www.theidioms.com/back-to-the-drawing-board/
https://knowyourphrase.com/back-to-the-drawing-board#
https://studiodesigns.com/art-and-craft/studio-designs-blog/history-of-drafting-tables-and-why-they-have-tilting-tops/
https://writingexplained.org/idiom-dictionary/back-to-the-drawing-board

Chapter Four: The Ball is in Your Court
https://www.dictionary.com/browse/the-ball-s-in-your-court
https://en.wikipedia.org/wiki/History_of_tennis
https://idioms.thefreedictionary.com/ball+is+in+your+court
https://www.grammar-monster.com/sayings_proverbs/the_ball_is_in_your_court.htm
https://www.theidioms.com/the-ball-is-in-your-court/
https://www.lifestyledijess.com/college-advice-and-lifestyle/what-it-means-when-a-guy-says-the-ball-is-in-your-court/
https://www.sportsrec.com/4616025/tennis-net-height-rules
https://www.usta.com/en/home/improve/tips-and-instruction/national/tennis-scoring-rules.html
https://stadiumfreak.com/facts-about-tennis-balls/#

Chapter Five: Bang Your Head Against a Wall
www.delpretemasonry.com/blog/brick-blog/fun-facts-brick/
https://www.dictionary.com/e/slang/brick-wall/
https://idioms.thefreedictionary.com/bang+head+against+a+brick+wall
https://idioms.thefreedictionary.com/bang+my+head+against+a+brick+wall
https://idioms.thefreedictionary.com/bang+your+head+against+a+brick+wall
https://motivationandlove.com/banging-your-head-against-a-brick-wall-quotes
https://www.oysterenglish.com/idiom-bang-ones-head-against-the-wall.html

Chapter Six: Barking up the Wrong Tree
https://en.wikipedia.org/wiki/Barking_up_the_wrong_tree
https://www.thefactsite.com/raccoon-facts/#
https://idiomorigins.org/origin/barking-up-the-wrong-tree
https://knowyourphrase.com/barking-up-the-wrong-tree
https://www.languagehumanities.org/where-did-the-phrase-barking-up-the-wrong-tree-originate.htm
https://www.phrases.org.uk/meanings/barking-up-the-wrong-tree.html
https://www.thesprucepets.com/dog-sense-of-smell-4776425

Chapter Seven: Be a Fly on the Wall
https://dictionary.cambridge.org/dictionary/english/fly-on-the-wall
https://easyscienceforkids.com/all-about-flies/# https://idioms.thefreedictionary.com/a+fly+on+the+wall
https://www.phrases.org.uk/meanings/139600.html

Chapter Eight: Beat Around the Bush
https://a-z-animals.com/animals/quail/#
https://www.gingersoftware.com/content/phrases/beat-around-the-bush/
https://www.theidioms.com/beat-around-the-bush/
https://idiomorigins.org/origin/beat-about-the-bush
https://justfunfacts.com/interesting-facts-about-shrubs/
https://knowyourphrase.com/beating-around-the-bush
https://www.languagehumanities.org/what-does-beat-around-the-bush-mean.htm

Chapter Nine Blockbuster
https://en.wikipedia.org/wiki/Blockbuster_bomb
https://en.wikipedia.org/wiki/Blockbuster_(retailer)
https://en.wikipedia.org/wiki/City_block
https://english.stackexchange.com/questions/387776/what-is-the-origin-of-the-term-blockbuster#
https://www.thefreedictionary.com/blockbuster
https://idioms.thefreedictionary.com/a+blockbuster
https://www.guinnessworldrecords.com/world-records/first-film-blockbuster
https://www.merriam-webster.com/dictionary/blockbuster
https://time.com/5776406/blockbuster-meaning/

Chapter Ten: Break the Ice
https://english-grammar-lessons.com/break-the-ice-meaning/#
https://www.dnr.state.mn.us/safety/ice/thickness.html
https://knowyourphrase.com/break-the-ice
hthps://www.oysterenglish.com/idiom-break-the-ice.html
https://www.phrases.org.uk/meanings/break-the-ice.html
http://tugboatrescue.com/tugboats.html#
https://wordhistories.net/2017/08/05/break-the-ice-origin/

Chapter Eleven: Butter Me Up
https://www.astroved.com/astropedia/en/gods/lord-vishnu
https://www.astroved.com/blogs/top-10-hindu-gods-and-their-favorite-foods#
www.foodreference.com/html/fbutter.html#
https://www.grammarly.com/blog/14-expressions-with-crazy-origins-that-you-would-never-have-guessed/

https://idioms.thefreedictionary.com/butter+me+up
https://idioms.thefreedictionary.com/butter+me+uptps://www.mmmenglish.com/2015/12/07/stop-buttering-me-up/#
tonsoffacts.com/29-fun-and-fascinating-facts-about-butter/

Chapter Twelve: Caught Red Handed
https://www.eastwestcollege.com/fun-facts-about-the-human-hand/#
https://en.wikipedia.org/wiki/Blood_red
https://www.gingersoftware.com/content/phrases/caught-red-handed/
https://idioms.thefreedictionary.com/a+red-letter+day
https://www.mentalfloss.com/article/33503/where-did-phrase-caught-red-handed-come
https://www.phrases.org.uk/meanings/caught-red-handed.html
https://www.phrases.org.uk/meanings/paint-the-town-red.html
https://www.thrillist.com/news/nation/caught-red-handed-meaning

Chapter Thirteen: Chicken Out
https://www.britannica.com/biography/Publius-Claudius-Pulcher
https://en.wikipedia.org/wiki/Chicken_(game)
https://english.stackexchange.com/questions/95494/etymology-of-the-phrase-chicken-out
https://www.factretriever.com/chicken-facts
https://idiomorigins.org/origin/chicken-out
https://idiomsandslang.com/game-of-chicken/
https://www.independent.co.uk/arts-entertainment/books/features/when-did-chicken-become-synonymous-with-being-afraid-9887896.html
https://www.idioms.online/chicken-out/
https://www.ldoceonline.com/dictionary/chicken-out

Chapter Fourteen: Cut Corners
https://thecontentauthority.com/blog/what-does-cutting-corners-mean
https://theconversation.com/these-are-the-characteristics-of-people-most-likely-to-cut-corners-at-work-69630
idiomic.com/cutting-corners
https://idiomorigins.org/origin/cut-cornersttps://improving-your-english.com/vocabulary/idioms/driving-idioms/#
https://literarydevices.net/strait-and-narrow/
https://nosweatshakespeare.com/quotes/famous/cutting-corners/

Chapter Fifteen: Cut Me Some Slack
https://dictionary.cambridge.org/dictionary/english/cut-some-slack
https://english-grammar-lessons.com/cut-me-some-slack-meaning/
https://howthingscompare.com/left-vs-right-scissors-is-there-a-difference/#
https://www.theidioms.com/cut-somebody-some-slack/#
https://www.merriam-webster.com/dictionary/give/cut%20(someone)%20some%20slack
https://thewordcounter.com/meaning-of-slack/#

Chapter Sixteen: Drive Me Up a Wall
https://www.allearsenglish.com/aee-647-drive-wall-mean-english/

https://www.chinahighlights.com/greatwall/fact/
https://climbingblogger.com/the-incredible-history-of-rock-climbing-as-a-sport/#
https://idioms.thefreedictionary.com/climb+the+wall
https://www.theidioms.com/drive-up-the-wall/
https://www.oysterenglish.com/idiom-drive-someone-up-the-wall.html
https://www.thoughtco.com/the-berlin-wall-28-year-history-1779495#

Chapter Seventeen: Fell off the Wagon
https://www.britannica.com/event/Social-Gospel
https://en.wikipedia.org/wiki/Wagon
https://fitrecovery.com/falling-off-the-wagon/
https://www.grunge.com/800998/where-did-the-phrase-fall-off-the-wagon-come-from/#
https://www.mentalfloss.com/article/640247/fall-off-the-wagon-phrase-origin

Chapter Eighteen: Flip the Bird
https://en.wikipedia.org/wiki/Middle_finger#
https://english.stackexchange.com/questions/64916/whats-the-origin-of-flipping-the-bird
https://www.theglobeandmail.com/news/world/where-did-the-term-flipping-the-bird-come-from/article544057/
https://www.merriam-webster.com/dictionary/flip%20(someone)%20the%20bird
https://oddfeed.net/the-short-history-of-flipping-the-bird/
https://owlcation.com/academia/25-Bird-Idioms-Explained-to-English-as-a-Second-Language-Learners#
https://www.reginacoeli.com/blog/goose-idioms.html
https://www.storypick.com/middle-finger-origins/

Chapter Nineteen: Get Up on the Wrong Side of Bed
https://christianity.stackexchange.com/questions/5160/why-are-people-traditionally-buried-facing-east#
https://www.finemortal.com/wake-up-on-the-wrong-side-of-the-bed/#
https://www.gingersoftware.com/content/phrases/wake-up-on-the-wrong-side-of-the-bed/
https://www.houstonmethodist.org/blog/articles/2021/dec/woke-up-on-the-wrong-side-of-the-bed-heres-how-to-not-let-it-ruin-your-day/
https://idiomorigins.org/origin/wrong-side-of-the-bed
https://illuminatingfacts.com/what-are-the-origins-of-the-saying-waking-up-on-the-wrong-side-of-the-bed/
https://www.independent.co.uk/life-style/health-and-families/health-news/the-wrong-side-of-the-bed-is-actually-a-thing-study-finds-a6749991.html
https://medium.com/the-collector/7-incredible-stories-behind-the-history-of-idioms-1f2aa4f2fea2
https://poosh.com/wrong-side-of-bed-mood/

Chapter Twenty: Glass Ceiling
https://builtin.com/diversity-inclusion/glass-ceiling
https://www.chicagobooth.edu/media-relations-and-communications/press-releases/the-glass-ceiling-three-reasons-why-it-still-exists-and-is-hurting-the-economy
https://en.wikipedia.org/wiki/Cranberry_glass
https://www.investopedia.com/terms/g/glass-ceiling.asp
https://kids.kiddle.co/Ceiling#
https://www.phrases.org.uk/meanings/glass-ceiling.html

https://www.techni-glassinc.com/2018/12/10-interesting-glass-facts/#

Chapter Twenty-One: Go Berserk
https://www.britannica.com/topic/berserker
https://www.collinsdictionary.com/dictionary/english/go-berserk
https://www.dictionary.com/browse/berserk
https://idioms.thefreedictionary.com/go+berserk
https://mythology.net/norse/norse-creatures/berserker/
https://www.snopes.com/fact-check/pluck-yew/
https://www.worldhistoryedu.com/12-common-myths-about-george-washington/

Chapter Twenty-Two: Going to Find Myself
https://en.wikipedia.org/wiki/Johari_window
https://en.wikipedia.org/wiki/Know_thyself
https://en.wikipedia.org/wiki/Paradigm_shift
https://www.enkiverywell.com/how-to-find-something-you-lost.html
https://idioms.thefreedictionary.com/find+oneself
https://www.goodreads.com/quotes/26227-to-find-yourself-think-for-yourself#
https://high5test.com/find-yourself-quiz/
https://www.merriam-webster.com/dictionary/find%20oneself
https://www.saybrook.edu/2014/10/01/10-01-14/

Chapter Twenty-Three: I'm Going to Get off my Soapbox
https://www.chagrinvalleysoapandsalve.com/blog/posts/what-is-the-origin-of-soap/
https://en.wikipedia.org/wiki/Don't_throw_the_baby_out_with_the_bathwater
https://www.grunge.com/668929/the-origin-behind-the-phrase-get-on-your-soapbox/
https://idioms.thefreedictionary.com/on+my+soapbox
https://www.thoughtco.com/history-of-microphones-1992144
https://www.thoughtco.com/stump-speech-definition-1773348

Chapter Twenty-Four: In the Nick of Time
https://en.wikipedia.org/wiki/History_of_ancient_numeral_systems
https://idioms.thefreedictionary.com/Nick+of+Time
https://grammarist.com/idiom/in-the-nick-of-time/
https://www.theidioms.com/in-the-nick-of-time/
https://www.phrases.org.uk/meanings/in-the-nick-of-time.html

Chapter Twenty-Five: In the Trenches
https://dictionary.cambridge.org/dictionary/english/trenches
https://idioms.thefreedictionary.com/In+the+Trenches
https://learnodo-newtonic.com/ww1-trenches-facts
https://www.merriam-webster.com/dictionary/the%20trenches
https://wikidiff.com/ditch/trench

Chapter Twenty-Six: It's Raining Cats and Dogs
https://en.wikipedia.org/wiki/Raining_cats_and_dogs

https://www.grammar-monster.com/sayings_proverbs/raining_cats_and_dogs.htm
https://idioms.thefreedictionary.com/In+the+Trenches
https://learnodo-newtonic.com/ww1-trenches-facts
https://www.merriam-webster.com/dictionary/the%20trenches
https://wikidiff.com/ditch/trench

Chapter Twenty-Six: It's Raining Cats and Dogs
https://en.wikipedia.org/wiki/Raining_cats_and_dogs
https://www.grammar-monster.com/sayings_proverbs/raining_cats_and_dogs.htm
https://www.konnecthq.com/rain-facts/#
https://www.loc.gov/everyday-mysteries/meteorology-climatology/item/what-is-the-origin-of-the-phrase-its-raining-cats-and-dogs/
https://www.phrases.org.uk/meanings/raining-cats-and-dogs.html
https://www.rd.com/list/rain-facts/

Chapter Twenty-Seven: Joshing Me
https://coinweek.com/us-coins/fact-or-myth-josh-tatum-and-racketeer-nickels/
https://www.dictionary.com/e/s/famous-names-inspired-common-words/#leotard
https://www.gingersoftware.com/content/phrases/joshing-me/
https://www.in2013dollars.com/us/inflation/1883
https://www.youridioms.com/en/idiom/joshing-me#

Chapter Twenty-Eight: Knock on Wood
https://en.wikipedia.org/wiki/Big_Brother_(Nineteen_Eighty-Four)
https://english-grammar-lessons.com/knock-on-wood-meaning/ttps://idioms.thefreedictionary.com/Walls%20have%20ears
https://en.wikipedia.org/wiki/Knocking_on_wood#
https://www.phrases.org.uk/meanings/knock-on-wood.html
https://propadv.com/1939-1945-world-war-ii/usa-ww2-careless-talk-propaganda-collection/1942-warning-walls-have-ears-be-careful-of-what-you-say/
https://www.rd.com/article/knock-on-wood-meaning/
https://www.refinery29.com/en-us/what-does-knock-on-wood-mean-history

Chapter Twenty-Nine: Let the Cat out of the Bag
https://en.wikipedia.org/wiki/Letting_the_cat_out_of_the_bag#
https://www.languagehumanities.org/what-are-the-origins-of-the-phrase-let-the-cat-out-of-the-bag.htm
https://www.mentalfloss.com/article/31180/whats-origin-let-cat-out-bag
https://www.phrases.org.uk/meanings/let-the-cat-out-of-the-bag.html
https://www.rd.com/article/let-the-cat-out-of-the-bag-origin/

Chapter Thirty: Money Laundering
https://en.wikipedia.org/wiki/Money_laundering
https://financialcrimeacademy.org/money-laundering-history-the-origin/

https://idioms.thefreedictionary.com/launder+money
https://theuijunkie.com/money-laundering-term/#

Chapter Thirty-One: The Oldest Trick in the Book
https://www.ancient-egypt-online.com/papyrus.html#
https://www.brainbubblegum.net/home/2017/8/6/the-oldest-trick-in-the-book
https://dictionary.cambridge.org/dictionary/english/oldest-trick-in-the-book
https://idioms.thefreedictionary.com/the+oldest+trick+in+the+book
https://www.mentalfloss.com/article/55202/whats-oldest-trick-book

Chapter Thirty-Two: On the Ball
https://en.wikipedia.org/wiki/List_of_sports_idioms
https://en.wikipedia.org/wiki/Rounders
https://idioms.thefreedictionary.com/on+the+ball
https://www.theidioms.com/on-the-ball/
https://www.oysterenglish.com/on-the-ball.html
https://www.phrases.org.uk/meanings/on-the-ball.html
https://www.redbull.com/us-en/history-of-soccer

Chapter Thirty-Three: On the Fence
https://bestoutdoorlivingproducts.com/fascinating-facts-about-fences/#
https://en.wikipedia.org/wiki/Joseph_Glidden#
https://english-grammar-lessons.com/sitting-on-the-fence-meaning/
https://www.gingersoftware.com/content/phrases/on-the-fence/
https://www.mamalisa.com/blog/robert-frosts-proverb-good-fences-make-good-neighbors/
https://www.phrases.org.uk/bulletin_board/38/messages/1787.html
https://www.usingenglish.com/reference/idioms/good+fences+make+good+neighbours.html#

Chapter Thirty-Four: Open a Can of Worms
https://www.acumence.com/the-history-of-canning-and-can-making/
https://castcountry.com/where-can-i-buy-worms-for-fishing
https://english-grammar-lessons.com/open-a-can-of-worms-meaning/ https://knowyourphrase.com/open-a-can-of-worms
https://www.languagehumanities.org/what-does-it-mean-to-open-a-can-of-worms.htm
https://www.mentalfloss.com/article/31039/how-did-term-open-can-worms-originate

Chapter Thirty-Five: A Piece of Cake
https://theartssociety.org/arts-news-features/10-amazing-facts-about-desserts#
https://idiomorigins.org/origin/piece-of-cake
https://idioms.thefreedictionary.com/as+easy+as+ABC
https://idioms.thefreedictionary.com/as+easy+as+pie
https://idioms.thefreedictionary.com/piece%20of%20cake
https://knowyourphrase.com/easy-as-pie
Shakespeare, William. Twelfth Night, Act II, Scene II. Quoted in shakespeare.mit.edu/twelfth_night/full.html
https://spoonuniversity.com/lifestyle/10-interesting-facts-about-pies-to-raise-your-pie-q#
https://www.floweraura.com/blog/15-exquisite-fun-and-interesting-facts-about-cake#

Chapter Thirty-Six: Proof is in the Pudding
https://en.wiktionary.org/wiki/pudding_time
https://english-grammar-lessons.com/the-proof-is-in-the-pudding-meaning/
https://htschool.hindustantimes.com/editorsdesk/knowledge-vine/where-does-the-phrase-the-proof-of-the-pudding-is-in-the-eating-originate-from
https://www.grunge.com/830155/the-dark-meaning-behind-the-phrase-the-proof-is-in-the-pudding/
https://justfunfacts.com/interesting-facts-about-pudding/
https://www.mentalfloss.com/article/635112/proof-is-in-the-pudding-origin

Chapter Thirty-Seven: The Rat Race
https://www.automatictrap.com/pages/101-rat-facts
https://en.wikipedia.org/wiki/Rat_race
https://ezinearticles.com/?Life-Is-A-Rat-Race?-And-What-Does-Rat-Race-Mean?&id=9078377
https://grammarist.com/idiom/rat-race/
https://idioms.thefreedictionary.com/rat+race
https://www.natgeokids.com/uk/discover/animals/general-animals/facts-about-rats/
https://www.urbandictionary.com/define.php?term=Dirty%20Rat

Chapter Thirty-Eight: Skeleton in the Closet
https://en.wikipedia.org/wiki/List_of_bones_of_the_human_skeleton https://www.joincake.com/blog/skeletons-in-the-closet/
https://www.mentalfloss.com/article/50405/what-origin-phrase-come-out-closet
https://www.merriam-webster.com/dictionary/skeletons%20in%20the/someone's%20closet
https://www.phrases.org.uk/meanings/skeleton-in-the-closet.html
https://www.thevintagenews.com/2016/06/30/renovation-benjamin-franklins-home-turns-dozens-bones/?edg-c=1
https://writingexplained.org/idiom-dictionary/skeletons-in-the-closet

Chapter Thirty-Nine: Spill the Beans
https://bosskitchen.com/20-interesting-facts-about-beans/
https://www.britannica.com/list/7-everyday-english-idioms-and-where-they-come-from
https://www.brownielocks.com/wordorigins.html
https://idioms.thefreedictionary.com/don't+know+beans+about
https://www.theidioms.com/spill-the-beans/
https://www.phrases.org.uk/meanings/spill-the-beans.html
https://www.rd.com/article/spill-the-beans-meaning/
https://www.wideopeneats.com/spill-the-beans/

Chapter Forty: Stabbed in the Back
https://www.annefrank.org/en/timeline/193/the-stab-in-the-back-legend/
https://thecontentauthority.com/blog/what-does-stab-someone-in-the-back-mean
https://en.wikipedia.org/wiki/Ides_of_March
https://en.wikipedia.org/wiki/Stab-in-the-back_myth
https://idioms.thefreedictionary.com/stab+in+the+back
https://www.theidioms.com/stab-in-the-back/
https://www.studysmarter.us/explanations/psychology/social-context-of-behaviour/personal-space/#

https://trypair.com/dating/types-of-hugs/#3_Squeeze_hug

Chapter Forty-One: Sweet Dreams
https://english.stackexchange.com/questions/134928/origin-of-the-greeting-sweet-dreams#
https://idioms.thefreedictionary.com/sweet+dreams
https://www.italki.com/en/article/NGnQTjgLN2dVPllYeeSGUx/sweet-dreams-7-idioms-about-sleep-and-dreams
https://thepleasantdream.com/how-long-do-dreams-last/
https://purlandtraining.com/2021/04/03/20-english-idioms-with-dream/
https://sleep.report/who-invented-the-bed/
https://www.songmeaningsandfacts.com/meaning-of-sweet-dreams-are-made-of-this-by-eurythmics/
https://www.urdupoint.com/dictionary/idioms/4781/sweet-dreams.html

Chapter Forty-Two: That's All She Wrote
https://www.funny-jokes.com/funny-christmas-trivia.htm#Christmas_Card_Trivia
https://grammarist.com/idiom/thats-all-she-wrote/
https://idioms.thefreedictionary.com/That's+all+she+wrote!
https://www.nationalww2museum.org/war/articles/mail-call-v-mail
https://www.phrases.org.uk/meanings/thats-all-she-wrote.html
https://short-fact.com/where-did-the-phrase-thats-all-she-wrote-come-from/#

Chapter Forty-Three: The Third Time's a Charm
https://www.allure.com/story/why-is-number-13-unlucky#
https://en.wikipedia.org/wiki/John_Babbacombe_Lee
https://en.wiktionary.org/wiki/third_time%27s_a_charm
https://www.gingersoftware.com/content/phrases/third-times-a-charm/
https://www.history.com/news/whats-so-unlucky-about-the-number-13
https://www.theidioms.com/third-times-a-charm/
https://learntalk.org/en/blog/where-did-the-saying-third-times-the-charm-come-from
https://www.mentalfloss.com/article/23266/13-reasons-people-think-number-13-unlucky

Chapter Forty-Four: Throw in the Towel
https://bbbofc.com/boxing-history
https://en.wikipedia.org/wiki/White_flag
https://www.idioms.online/throw-in-the-towel/
https://idioms.thefreedictionary.com/throw+in+the+towel
https://knowyourphrase.com/throw-in-the-towel
https://www.phrases.org.uk/meanings/throw-in-the-towel.html
https://promotions247.com.au/blogs/seo-blog-post/interesting-and-unknown-facts-about-towel#

Chapter Forty-Five: Throw Under the Bus
https://busfoundation.org/answers-on-questions/often-asked-what-does-throw-under-the-bus-mean.html
https://en.wikipedia.org/wiki/Throw_to_the_wolves#
https://en.wikipedia.org/wiki/Throw_under_the_bus
https://www.funkidslive.com/learn/top-10-facts/top-10-facts-about-busses/

https://www.merriam-webster.com/words-at-play/why-do-we-throw-someone-under-the-bus
https://philmckinney.com/being-thrown-under-the-bus-the-dilemma-of-blame/
https://www.yahoo.com/lifestyle/mysterious-origin-key-lime-pie-192930215.html

Chapter Forty-Five: The Life Saver
https://en.wikipedia.org/wiki/Life_Savers
https://interestingfactsworld.com/life-savers-facts.html
hhttps://life-savers.fandom.com/wiki/History_of_Life_Savers
https://www.mentalfloss.com/article/77729/10-things-you-might-not-know-about-life-savershttps://solvedir.com/faq/why-is-there-a-hole-in-the-middle-of-a-lifesaver-candy/
https://www.thoughtco.com/history-of-life-savers-candy-4076664

Chapter Forty-Six: M&M's
https://en.wikipedia.org/wiki/Forrest_Mars_Sr.
https://en.wikipedia.org/wiki/M%26M%27s
https://www.thefactsite.com/facts-about-m-and-ms/
https://www.history.com/news/the-wartime-origins-of-the-mm
https://historynewsnetwork.org/article/140489
https://kidadl.com/facts/what-were-original-m-and-m-colors-curious-candy-facts-that-kids-will-adore

Chapter Forty-Seven: The MoonPie
https://www.enewscourier.com/archives/moonpie-trivia/article_92db0148-3666-55c4-9317-84f8e832baa9.html
https://en.wikipedia.org/wiki/Moon_Pie
https://www.mashed.com/716322/the-untold-truth-of-moonpie/
https://moonpie.com/about

Chapter Forty-Eight: Neapolitan Ice Cream
https://astronautfoods.com/blogs/news/the-sweet-history-of-astronaut-ice-cream https://bestiesicecream.com/blog/8dagdjn1rrqi0e39v6srm425qx8sm6 https://en.wikipedia.org/wiki/Flag_of_Italy
https://en.wikipedia.org/wiki/Neapolitan_ice_cream
https://www.foodreference.com/html/f-neapolitan-ice-cream.html https://www.popsugar.com/food/Neapolitan-Ice-Cream-Origin-11674054

Chapter Forty-Nine: Popcorn
https://www.airfungames.com/party-rental-resources/popcorn-first-discovered
https://www.bbc.co.uk/bitesize/articles/zn8g3j6
https://www.cretors.com
https://en.wikipedia.org/wiki/Cretors
https://en.wikipedia.org/wiki/Popcorn
https://www.popcorn.org/All-About-Popcorn/History-of-Popcorn

Chapter Fifty: The Tootsie Roll
https://clickamericana.com/topics/food-drink/tootsie-rolls-americas-favorite-candy-1955 https://en.wikipedia.org/wiki/Tootsie_Roll
https://www.mashed.com/252208/the-untold-truth-of-tootsie-rolls/ https://www.smithsonianmag.com/smart-news/tootsie-rolls-were-wwii-energy-bars-180962202/
https://time.com/4230820/tootsie-roll-history-origins-name-120th-anniversary/
https://www.wearethemighty.com/mighty-history/marines-saved-candy-sky/#

www.ingramcontent.com/pod-product-compliance
Lightning Source LLC
Chambersburg PA
CBHW051007140626
46546CB00016B/1068